THANKS FOR
BLASTING BY !

Autism
Every Day

Over 150 Strategies Lived and Learned
by a Professional Autism Consultant
with 3 Sons on the Spectrum

Alyson Beytien, M.S.

Autism Every Day

All marketing and publishing rights guaranteed to
and reserved by:

FUTURE HORIZONS INC.

721 W. Abram Street
Arlington, Texas 76013
800-489-0727
817-277-0727
817-277-2270 (fax)
E-mail: info@FHautism.com
www.FHautism.com

ISBN-13: 978-1-935274-50-6

Publisher's Cataloging-In-Publication Data
(Prepared by The Donohue Group, Inc.)

Beytien, Alyson.
  Autism every day : over 150 strategies lived and learned by a professional autism
consultant with 3 sons on the spectrum / Alyson Beytien.

  p. ; cm.

  Includes index.
  ISBN: 978-1-935274-50-6

  1. Autistic children--Care--Popular works. 2. Autism--Popular works. 3. Autism in
children--Popular works. I. Title.

RC553.A88 B49 2011
616.85/882

Printed in USA

To Spenc[...]chary[...]
who love me even whe[...]the[...]
Love you more[...]

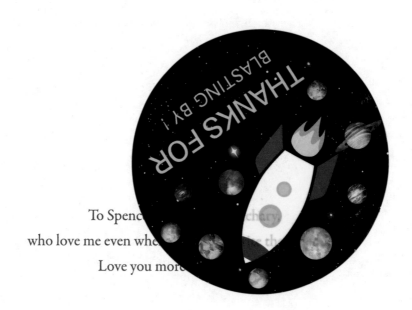

ACKNOWLEDGEMENTS

I have been the recipient of a substantial amount of support and encouragement in the past 17 years. This book is written because of that support.

My family and I are forever grateful to Kathryn Makeever, Jenny Potanos and Jane Freiburger. Any "success" our family has experienced started with their support. In the early days of the diagnosis of autism, these amazing professionals showed us how to help our boys and provided endless hours of encouragement, knowledge, and empathy. When I grow up, I want to be just like them!

Patti Boheme and the staff at Little Friends, Inc. provided the structure and training we needed to be our boys' best teachers. Patti's guidance and commitment to individuals with autism inspired me not only to work with my own children but also with others.

Kathy Gould taught me how to give a presentation, navigate a state's political system, and persevere in what is right even when it seems impossible. And how to get lost in the back roads of the Midwest!

I have had the incredible privilege of knowing the top experts in the field of autism. Dr. Cathy Pratt, Carol Gray, Dr. Richard Simpson, and Dr Brenda Smith-Myles have all encouraged me, guided me, and generously shared their knowledge and time over the years. I am very thankful for their support and still want to have their autograph!

When Diane Twachtman-Cullen asked me to write a column for the *Autism Spectrum Quarterly* magazine six years ago, I didn't believe that my stories of life with my three boys would be that interesting or helpful to people. She has constantly told me I'm wrong! Her kind editing of my column and encouragement over the years have made this book possible. She has carved out time in her busy schedule to be a thoughtful editor and friend and I am truly thankful. When it came time to consider a Foreword for the book, Diane was my immediate choice. I am so grateful she agreed to write it.

My family has been my sounding board, my critic and my cheerleader. I am blessed with supportive brothers, sisters-in-law, nieces, nephews, aunts, uncles, cousins, and more, who always let me tell the latest funny story. Thanks for laughing with me and not laughing at me!

I have been blessed with parents who always taught me that I was capable of doing anything. They encouraged me throughout my life to work hard, laugh frequently, and show compassion for others. They learned the word "autism" and became stellar grandparents and caregivers to my boys. They have given me and my family the unconditional love needed to survive and thrive with ASD.

I adore my husband. I cannot imagine my world without him. He has been my publisher, editor, critic, friend, and groupie for years! He has pushed me and supported me in completing my graduate work, doing presentations around the country, and helping other families. He may grumble a bit when I'm on the phone at midnight with a family in crisis, but he's always the first to hand me the phone! I love you beyond words, sweetheart.

Of course, the only reason there is a book in your hands, and you're reading this gushing litany of appreciation is because of my boys. Beyond all the visual systems, therapies, and educational interventions, I wanted my boys to know that I loved them more than anything. They are wonderful individuals and their happiness is my definition of "success." I am so glad to be their mother. I love their sense of humor, their views of life, and their ability to keep me focused on what truly matters in this world. I am so proud of them and hope they will forever feel my love. Thanks guys, for letting me share our story.

TABLE OF CONTENTS

PART I–Characteristics of Autism

PART II–Education

PART III–Family Life

PART IV–Community Interactions

FOREWORD

I first met Alyson Beytien at a dinner party in Pittsburgh, Pennsylvania approximately eight years ago. In those days, having multiple children on the autism spectrum was still a pretty rare circumstance. So, I didn't know what to expect. Would she be reluctant to share her experiences as the mother of three boys with ASD? Would she be beyond frazzled by the additional responsibilities that "ASD times three" would undoubtedly add to a young mother's life? Would the stressors of parenting children with unique needs cause her to view the glass as "half empty" instead of "half full"?

I am happy to report that the answer to these questions is *none of the above!* What I found, instead, was a charming, upbeat (the word *indefatigable* comes to mind!), dynamo who gave new meaning to the term *supermom*. And, as waves of laughter spilled over from Alyson's end of the table, I learned that for her the glass is much more than "half full"; it is indeed over-brimming!

Fast forward two years. Starfish Specialty Press, LLC was about to launch its Magajournal®, *Autism Spectrum Quarterly (ASQ)*. We were looking for a mom or dad to write a regular column about the topsy-turvy world of parenting a child on the autism spectrum. Alyson immediately came to mind. If truth be told, she was my *first* and *only* choice, for I knew that regardless of her subject matter, she would do it justice, and then some. She did not disappoint! It's been seven years since Alyson's inaugural column, "You too?! Common Stories from an Uncommon Parent," made its debut. And, to this moment, it remains one of our most popular regular features.

As editor-in-chief of *ASQ*, I have had the pleasure (a word I rarely use in this context!) of editing Alyson's articles. A gifted storyteller, Alyson is able to turn the mundane into the extraordinary, and deliver life's important messages in ways that resonate and linger. While known and very much appreciated for her "lemons into lemonade" humorous style, she is equally at home addressing serious—even pro-foundly deep—topics.

In *Autism Every Day*, Alyson shares with her readers many of her best-loved stories and some brand new ones. Those familiar with Alyson's "all it takes is all you've got" approach to parenting will no doubt be thrilled to re-visit her guys, and to have the collection in a single volume. Those new to her work will find her wit, wisdom, and style both engaging and refreshing. More than that, they will find the Beytien family's *esprit de corps*, which Alyson so beautifully conveys, inspirational.

Readers will find within the pages of this book more than just a collection of beautifully rendered stories that will sometimes provoke laughter, and other times tears. They will also find a roadmap for living life to the fullest, for after all of the stories are told, it is Alyson's message that will endure—that the secret to handling *autism, every day,* is to fully accept and respect your children for who they are, and more than that, to celebrate their quirks as you rejoice in and honor their gifts.

Diane Twachtman-Cullen, Ph.D., CCC-SLP
Editor-in-Chief, *Autism Spectrum Quarterly*

INTRODUCTION

"Hello, we have autism . . . "

I find it difficult to introduce myself to people. Because of work and civic engagements with my husband, I am frequently required to introduce myself and my family. The dilemma: Do I announce our autism immediately and wait for the gasp? "Hi, I'm Alyson Beytien and I have three sons with autism." (gasp! silence! stunned look!) I've always wanted to be introduced as "Stunningly beautiful and amazingly intelligent," but that will take a lot more sleep and plastic surgery!

Introducing my sons is more complicated than a single sentence can accomplish. Spencer is 20 years old, 6'1" tall, 150 lbs., and has a diagnosis of Asperger's syndrome. He understands most sarcastic comments and college humor, has difficulty initiating conversation, loves video games, anime, and used to eat only white food. Joshua is

19 years old, 6' tall, 160 lbs., and has a diagnosis of high-functioning autism (although on any given day, he is not functioning well at all!). Josh is currently interested in mythical creatures, wild animals, loves to surf the internet, read, draw pictures, eat at Burger King, and needs to know his schedule for the next six months or he has an emotional breakdown. Zachary is 17 years old, 6'3" tall, 190 lbs., and has a diagnosis of autism. He loves Burger King, wants to do anything his brothers do, uses an augmentative communication device, gives great kisses, and loves to swim. Zach struggles with anxiety and aggression, and works harder than anyone I know to participate with other kids.

And even having told you that, you cannot truly understand my family. The boys have made great progress in their ability to enjoy and live their lives. Each day I am amazed at what they do. Zachary spontaneously said, "love you Mama" just two months ago. Would the incredible joy of that moment be understood by the casual person who wants to know who we are? Joshua is the most loving, funny, "quirky" guy, and says the most outrageous things! Will his Sunday School teacher be able to see the humor in his comments if she doesn't know the way he thinks? Spencer has come so far that I question whether to tell his diagnosis to the college kids who come to our home. But if I don't, and he says something socially inappropriate, will they ever come back?

My boys' disability affects every aspect of our lives, but it is not the defining description of who we are as a family, or as individuals for that matter. I am not just the mom of three sons with autism—I could also say that I am a quilter, gardener, scrapbooking fiend, pianist, consultant, educator, wife, sister, daughter, and friend. If I used those descriptions of myself, would my introduction still make others gasp and give me stunned looks?! Just as my sons are also people beyond their autism, so am I a person beyond being their mom. But if you don't know about the autism, do you truly know about me?

My husband and I have worked with our sons to help them understand their disability. To know the words and to understand the ways in which their disability affects their lives. Not to give them an excuse nor a label. This information has provided a platform for them to tell us how they think and process their world, and an opportunity for us to discuss with them how others might think or feel differently than they do. We began discussing their autism with them when our first son, Spencer, was in the fourth grade. For a while after that, he introduced himself as "Spencer Beytien. I have Asperger's syndrome and my brothers have LOTS of autism." That sure got a lot of attention! And Joshua frequently introduces himself alongside his current interest—"Hi, I'm Josh Beytien. Do you like Big Boy 4-6-6-4 steam locomotives built in the Roanoke shops of Virginia in the 1930's?"

After people meet me, I frequently hear the comment that I am "not what they expected." Makes you wonder what they *did* expect of a mom who has three kids with autism. (Or any of us moms for that matter!) A straitjacket? Bitterness? Dark circles under my eyes? (Oh, wait, I DO have those!) Sometimes I wonder if everyone will look at us or treat us differently if my introduction includes the diagnosis? Will they look for problems that aren't there? Or, without knowing the diagnosis, will they have the understanding to forgive the social indiscretions? I'm frequently uncertain of the best route to take.

The reality is that I am simply a mom. I have good days and difficult days. I cry, laugh, worry, and live like everyone else—just more intensely and frequently than most! I want to make the best decisions

XX   AUTISM EVERY DAY

I can for my boys. I want them to be happy, healthy, and know that they are loved intensely. Stress, Laughter and Joy live side by side in our home—and their names are Spencer, Joshua, and Zachary.

This book is a compilation of essays, some of which were published in the *Autism Spectrum Quarterly* magazine. The stories and strategies cover our 18 years (and counting!) of living with autism. My wonderful husband has tried to get me to assemble this collection for some time. He finally wore me down. If you don't find anything in this book helpful, blame him. If you do find some of my ideas helpful, then remember that I'm "stunningly beautiful and amazingly intelligent."

I know that many of you struggle with the same issues I do. I hope this book will be an opportunity to share in the struggles and joys of raising our kids with autism. I believe that by sharing some of our family's challenges and successes, you will recognize your own and know that you are not alone. I hope that this book will provide you with a chuckle to brighten your day and a strategy to make your life easier! So, by way of introduction: "Hello, we have autism . . . "

PART I

Characteristics of Autism

CHAPTER 1

Foreshadowing: Early Signs of Autism

Prologue: In January of 1994, I wrote the following letter to my extended family.

Spencer was about to turn three years old, Joshua was 20 months old, and Zachary was two months old. We had just moved to a new town, new neighborhood, new home, and we did not know that autism would be part of our lives in the coming months. And email and the internet didn't exist!

Dear Family,

Thanks so much for the letter! It truly was the highlight of my week and I am going to try to reciprocate the feeling by writing to you. Provided, of course, that Zachary will sleep more than twenty minutes (not his habit), and Joshua will not climb all over me and scream (definitely his habit), and Spencer will leave both of them alone (guess what his habit is). Batman just came on TV, so maybe I can get them to sit still for a while.

The boys are definitely keeping me hopping. Last Friday was a day from hell. Spencer got up at 5:30, then Joshua a few minutes later, so I was not coherent enough to start the day. They managed to spill two glasses of milk at breakfast, and pour syrup over the table. Then, when I sat down to nurse Zachary, Spencer and Joshua went upstairs to play. After a while, I realized that I hadn't heard any sound from them. I went upstairs (carrying the nursing baby) to find Spencer behind the cradle, snipping away at the dust ruffle with Craig's moustache scissors. I sent him downstairs, answered the ringing phone, then came downstairs myself. Only to find the two of them in the laundry room, pouring laundry soap all over each other. At this point, I had to lay Zachary down, which made him unhappy because he wasn't finished eating, so he started screaming. Took both boys upstairs to bathe (do you know how difficult it is to get detergent out of hair?), put clean clothes on them, and sent them downstairs again. I put a Bugs Bunny video in and went to sweep up the laundry room and hallway. Zachary was still crying at this point. After cleaning up, I realized that they weren't in the family room watching the video. I went upstairs again to find them in the guest room, emptying all six drawers of unused children's clothes, throwing them all over the room, and laughing gleefully. At this point, I am ready to do bodily harm to somebody! ☺ I sent Spencer to his room, took Joshua downstairs, and came downstairs to calm down and finish feeding Zachary. When I went back upstairs to talk to Spencer, I found that he had emptied all of his dresser drawers also. I called Craig and told him not to be surprised if he came home from work and found his children in the snow because something needed to chill them out! Craig asked if he should bring home chocolate—smart man.

Later that day, after I tried to put Joshua down for a nap (which is something that never really happens), I came downstairs to find the toaster out of the cupboard and plugged in. A chair was next to the freezer (Spencer's favorite food is a waffle, and it is in the freezer) and there was a waffle in the toaster. The toaster was actually cooking, a fork and knife was on the table, along with a bottle of syrup and a very happy Spencer looked at me and said, "I did it Mama. I did it!" I know that is supposed to thrill me, and truthfully it does, but it also makes me wonder what else he will do when I'm not around!

Spencer is definitely in his three's. He has become a trifle defiant and disobedient. I am reading every parenting book on discipline that I can find. He seems to have no remorse when he does something wrong. He jabbers constantly, but usually none of it makes any sense. I could have sworn he was talking much better a few months ago. I'm thinking of having him tested next month for his verbal skills. If he is behind, then the school district will put him into preschool. He is very loving towards Zachary—wants to hold him, and is always telling me when Zach is crying (which is often!). He absolutely LOVES the Mighty Morphing Power Rangers (do you have that TV show where you live?) and is constantly asking to watch it. Between that and Bugs Bunny, we have a very interesting viewing schedule.

Joshua reminds me of a bear—he is large in size (almost as big as Spencer) and very passionate in temperament. He is either very angry, very happy, very funny, very irritating—you get the picture. He loves Bugs Bunny, *101 Dalmations*, or anything with a dog or bunny in it. He will watch the movies and literally stand two feet from the TV and dance with happiness. It is the funniest thing to watch. He is currently into matchbox cars and carries two of them around with him constantly. He also likes to sleep with his cars. He is an independent child—he doesn't like to have Spencer mess with him or his toys. He has gotten very adept at pushing Spencer away, hitting Spencer when he bugs him, and he also tackles Spencer to throw him to the ground. He is a very physical child. He loves to snuggle in bed with us, to sit next to us or on top of us, anywhere where he can be touching us. His favorite thing is to hold your hand while he is watching cartoons—strange, isn't it? He loves to read books, and we read *Brown Bear, Brown Bear* about 20 times a day. He never seems to tire of it. Joshua seems to be the most affected by Zachary's arrival. He has recently begun to climb on the couch when I am nursing Zach and body slam me, or whine and cry and try to push me off the couch. Not a really pleasant experience, but I'm hoping it's a phase.

Zachary—well, at two months old, he doesn't have much of

a personality yet. He looks a lot like Spencer in his physical features. He is a catnapper, but does sleep pretty well at night. He struggles from 6:30-10:30 every night, crying, arching his back, and screaming. Craig is holding him right now to give me a break and let me write this letter. We put some James Taylor on the CD and Craig is dancing and singing with Zach. He seems to be calming down. He is focusing on our faces now, and we even get a few smiles every now and then. He has dimples, which is good because he looks so much like his brothers, it might be the only way to tell them apart!

That's it for the excitement in our lives. Craig is working hard, I'm surviving the kids, and we wish we could see you more often. Take care and give everyone a kiss for us!

Love, Alyson

It's easy to look back on our children's lives after we have a diagnosis and wonder why we didn't see the signs. For many families like us, a lack of experience with autism and child development prevents us from noticing the delays. I don't remember even hearing the word "autism" until a professional said it in relation to Josh. With the increased attention that autism has been given in the media in the past ten years, many parents are questioning their children's development earlier than ever before. This is a good thing! It would be much better to have a child evaluated for autism and find out that there is nothing wrong, than to go months or years without getting the early intervention that is needed.

I was actually relieved when Joshua, and then Spencer, was

diagnosed with autism. I had been deeply worried that their behaviors and challenges indicated that I was a terrible mother and parent. Knowing that there was a reason for the overwhelming stress I felt allowed me to provide a more appropriate environment and response.

STRATEGIES FOR DIAGNOSIS

1. Evaluate Language and Communication.

The majority of children seen for an autism evaluation have language delays. This is because language is something we *notice*. We are a world of verbalists—and if a child isn't communicating with verbal language we notice it immediately. Individuals with autism are concrete, literal thinkers. They are visual, kinesthetic learners. They have to see it, touch it, and experience it in order to understand it. Individuals with Asperger's Syndrome and high-functioning autism have verbal language. But they struggle to communicate effectively. They also may not have any other form of communication—gestures, facial expressions, and body postures may be very limited. People communicate through multiple forms, not just verbal language. But the presence of some verbal language typically delays a diagnosis.

2. Observe Social Interaction.

Social interactions and language are intimately connected. Without appropriate verbal language, people struggle to interact socially. Without an ability to understand other people's perspectives, social interactions are stilted and awkward. If social interactions are limited, then language does not develop appropriately.

Individuals with autism spectrum disorders are easily overwhelmed by their senses, often unable to screen out distractions. This not only limits their ability to communicate effectively, but also contributes to the misreading of social cues, social situations, and a misunderstanding of the expected behaviors within a given environment. A person with autism may be highly skilled in computer repair, but they will never get a job or keep a job if their social skills are inappropriate. Teaching appropriate social interaction skills is critical for lifelong success and personal fulfillment.

3. Schedule Evaluations and Assessment.

If a child is exhibiting any of the early signs of autism, an evaluation should be scheduled. Assessments should include specific language testing, observation of social interactions, assessment of sensory processing, and a behavioral assessment. At this time, we can only diagnose autism by observation. There are standardized assessment tools that assist in quantifying the observed behaviors and determining whether the person has an autism spectrum disorder. Ensuring that the assessment is done with a full team will provide the most comprehensive insight and appropriate diagnosis.

CHAPTER 2

The Gathering:
Passions and Obsessions

A friend of mine was asked in a job interview, "What piece of trivia do you know, and why is it important to you?" When she related this story, she told me that she could not think of a single bit of trivia.

Obviously, she doesn't have a child with autism!

Hang out with a child with autism for any length of time and you'll learn things you never thought you needed (or wanted?) to know. Our kids could easily beat Ken Jennings at Jeopardy on the subject of their interests! Some might even be able to calculate the perfect odds for which suitcase holds the million dollars on Deal or No Deal. Not that we'll ever see our kids on the game shows—they'd never survive the screaming audience. But our kids certainly do know "stuff"—trivia, tidbits, and pieces of information that other people don't know (and probably don't care about).

My boys' intense interests have filled my life with all kinds of trivia over the years. For instance, I know that the Big Boy 4-6-6-4 steam locomotive was built in the Roanoke, Virginia Railroad shops in the 1930's. I know that the Charizard Pokemon character has a Fire power and can fly. I also know the names of the different species of whales, sharks, and warthogs, and that a peccary is a type of wild pig indigenous to Arizona and New Mexico. I can quote Disney movies, and sing all the songs verbatim! I know which Paleolithic period the Allosaurs lived in; what their diet consisted of; and their size in comparison to the T-Rex. I know that the red Mystic Force Power Ranger morphs into a Phoenix; that SpongeBob's pet snail is named Gary; and that Kool-Aid was invented in Hastings, Nebraska.

The intense interests or passions of our ASD kids are often viewed as weird or problematic. Granted, not many people want to have in-depth discussions on electrical towers, vegetables, or Neanderthals. But, to me, such passions are directly connected to each individual's personal interests. I don't want to have deep discussions about Brett Favre and the Green Bay Packers, but the majority of people where I live think this is a subject that everyone wants to discuss.

Importantly, when it comes to kids with ASD, you need to know that it's not enough just to KNOW about dragons, African mammals, and Yu-Gi-Oh characters. They have to also COLLECT their special things too! When Josh was eight and Zachary seven, their passion for trains knew no bounds. They read books on trains, watched two-hour videos on steam locomotives, and drew pictures of engines for hours at a time. We worked our family vacations around where the nearest railroad museum was located. While at the National Railroad Museum in Green Bay, Wisconsin, Joshua asked one of the engineers conducting our tour whether the particular engine we were looking at was a Shay or a Mikado engine. The engineer looked shocked at the question from such a young child, but proceeded to answer it. (It was a Shay, in case you were interested!) He then carried on a five-minute, in-depth conversation with Josh about steam locomotives. At the time, we thought Josh's knowledge was sketchy at best, until the engineer said to us, "I'd hire him on the spot if he were 16!"

The boys collect everything they can about their current interests. Thank heavens for Ebay and the Internet where we can search for the rare Obelisk the Tormentor Yu-gi-Oh card or the latest Ertl Thomas Engine. Currently, in my home, we have collections of Pokemon figures, Bionicles, Cars miniatures, dinosaur figures, Thomas the Tank Engines (in wood, metal, plastic, HO scale and O scale), LGB trains, BBC channel videos, anime DVDs, dinosaur books, colored markers, Super Balls, swords, dragon figures, thousands of Legos, and fabric.

FABRIC, you're thinking? Well, that's MY collection. Nothing is dearer to a quilter's heart than her fabric stash. I add to it whenever I can—even if I don't have a specific project in mind. I can't resist the colors and patterns. When I travel, I always try to find time to locate the nearest quilt store so I can add to my collection. Owning a few yards of a fabulous color or beautiful print gives me a bit of joy—a pop of pleasure.

Kind of like owning another Thomas the Tank Engine!

STRATEGIES FOR DEALING
WITH SPECIAL INTERESTS

1. Control the Access, Not the Interest.

Everyone gets to choose their interest or hobby. But we don't get to choose to engage in that hobby all the time. Helping the person with autism learn where and when it is appropriate to engage in their passion is critical. Especially if the special interest isn't necessarily age appropriate. For example, Joshua still loves owning the Thomas the Tank Engine trains. We've taught him that his interest in Thomas is fine, but needs to be part of his life at home, not at work or school. He can talk to us about Thomas, but other teenagers probably won't want to discuss Thomas.

2. Collections Are Perfect Reward Systems.

(I don't really need to explain this, do I?)

3. Teach a Variety of Conversation Topics.

Some individuals need to learn to discuss something other than their particular interest. A visual structure can frequently help support this learning. We used "talk tickets" to restrict the number of times that Spencer could talk about Transformers. Initially, Spencer had about 20 "tickets" that he could give us when he wanted to talk about Transformers. (Believe me, I was seriously tired of talking about Transformers!) Then we started to reduce the number of Transformer tickets and give him tickets on other topics we knew he could engage in. Eventually, he had only one Transformer ticket each day—and he frequently didn't even use it!

CHAPTER 3

Eat, Drink, and Be Picky: Eating Issues

Nothing can make me feel more horrible about my parenting skills than seeing a Food Pyramid—you know, the poster that's in every school building, cafeteria, and doctor's office that indicates how much of each food group your body needs to grow and develop; the one that's supposed to visually show you the inadequacy of what you're feeding your children; the poster that doesn't look *anything* like the diet of most humans! Because, seriously, who *really* eats 10-12 servings of vegetables or fruits each day? I know I don't.

To Each His Own

Our boys have always had food issues. I was always the mom who made different meals for everybody in my family because they wouldn't eat the same thing. I even rationalized that ketchup really was a vegetable serving. I would bring our own food to family gatherings because my boys wouldn't eat anything being served. I even lied to my pediatrician (and my mother-in-law!) about what I made for dinner. And I packed the same food in one of my son's lunch bag for seven years because he wouldn't eat anything in the cafeteria but Cheetos dipped in peanut butter.

As a young child, Spencer would eat only white food—bread, Cheerios, French fries, and waffles. Joshua would eat only crunchy, salty foods; and Zachary would eat Jack's Frozen Pepperoni Pizza, Cheerios, and chicken nuggets ONLY from Burger King. They also wouldn't eat cookies, ice cream, or chocolate, which should have made me ecstatic and pompous, but children who don't eat chocolate? How does that happen?

Food Wars

I consulted a nutritionist numerous times over the course of the years. The first one told me to offer three healthy meals and snacks per day, and said that if the boys didn't eat I should let them go hungry. She assured me that children will not starve themselves—the boys would eventually eat the food I prepared. So I stood firm with the offer-only-healthy-food advice and Spencer went FIVE days without eating, before I gave up and handed him a bowl of Cheerios! I just couldn't handle my child looking like a war refugee.

I worked with another nutritionist who helped me create a visual system that would enable the boys to predict what food they would eat on different days. I spent days creating a consistent weekly menu (spaghetti on Monday, tacos on Tuesday, etc.). I built in rewards for each attempt at eating—a Thomas movie if Joshua would eat chicken; computer time for Spencer if he would drink a glass of water; a new train for Zach if he would eat a vegetable. I even used the colors of the rainbow to entice the boys into eating healthy foods. For example, if they ate a food that was a color on the rainbow every two days they would get a prize out of the prize box. Unfortunately, the visuals and rules were so complicated even an IRS agent wouldn't have been able to understand them! The behavior program was a total failure. Worse yet, it cost me hours of time to create the visuals, and hundreds of dollars in rewards!

I have tried numerous other behavior plans, reward systems, and visual supports in my attempts to change the boys' eating habits. The stress of constantly trying to get them to eat something healthy was intense. During one of the food management programs, Spencer told me, on an hourly basis, that I was "ruining his life." Joshua screamed at me when I announced it was time for dinner, "You are an angry buffalo!" and Zachary would start hitting me. (Add to this the remarks from my husband!)

During one of my feeble attempts at changing his diet, Joshua wrote me the following note:

Dear Mom

I feel sad and lonely and no one loves me and they didn't give me anything, they didn't take me places everyday. If I don't have soda, popcorn, fries, butter bread and more food, I'll never make my days and holidays. Why do they care? Why? Does everyone don't love me?

Write this: _____

"Write this" was Joshua's way of telling me he wanted a response in writing.

My response:

> Dear Joshua, I love you very much. Everyone loves you. Because I love you, I want you to eat healthy foods. That's why we are changing our foods at home. We will still have holidays. Change is hard, but eating healthy will make everyone feel better. I know that you can try to be happy about new, healthy foods like vegetables and meat.

Josh's verbal response: "That's nice but I love original foods."

On another day:

> Dear Mom,
> I feel angry because I don't want cheese in my snack and I don't want green stuff and chop in my lunch.
> Love Josh.
> PS. It's my birthday today, so no celery, no cheese, no chicken!
> Cheeseburgers. Yes.
> Cheese sandwiches. Yes.
> Cheetosticks. Yes
> Carrots. Yes
> Cheerios. Yes

An Emerging Truce

Food is such an intimate, cultural, emotional subject. Feeding our children is a critical need for all moms. When you add the emotional issue of wanting to give your child something—ANYTHING—that will make him happy, the challenge of feeding a child who eats only chicken nuggets and potato chips can be exhausting. And feeding them is so *daily*! I would feel frustrated and inadequate three times or more per day—every time I was supposed to be a "good mom" and feed them carrots and spinach. I was also embarrassed. I just knew that the teachers were talking about me in the lunchroom when they saw that Zachary's lunch consisted of Froot Loops cereal, Tostito chips, and lemonade.

It's not as if I'm a lousy cook—the irony is, I LOVE to cook! I am a Food Network junkie. I love to try new recipes, bake fancy desserts, and cook for parties. But I was a failure at enticing my children to try something new. They would scream and cry if a new food was even on the table, let alone near their plate.

I told myself that changing their eating habits didn't have to be at the top of the intervention priority list. The boys were growing, rarely ill, and very active. But this was just rationalization and emotional survival on my part (of course, that's not necessarily a bad thing!). A part of me empathized with them because I remember eating Cheerios every single morning for four years of high school! I didn't eat a varied diet until I was in my twenties. How was I going to convince the boys that broccoli tasted great, when I hadn't liked it until I was 26?

When the guys entered their teen years, two things changed. They slept more than six hours a night, and they were willing to try new foods. Not a lot of different foods, but some. Spencer told me,

"I think my taste buds are growing up." Zachary, at 17, ate almost everything we put in front of him, including cheeseburgers, coconut shrimp, pot stickers, and salad. AND broccoli! I was soooo proud! And once, Joshua asked if we could stop at Dairy Queen because he wanted a vanilla ice cream cone. Just vanilla—but hey! He had *never* eaten ice cream in his life! This was a shining moment for me. And Spencer chose salmon as his birthday dinner this year—the same boy who would eat only four foods, now asks for fish and shrimp!

The best intervention for their eating habits has turned out to be time and opportunity. Oh sure, a little coaxing on my part probably helped. But mostly, the change occurred with the passage of time, a lessening of rigidity and anxiety, and an increase in their social skills. So although my food behavior interventions failed, I like to think that all my *other* interventions have succeeded. And that is a rationalization that I can sink my teeth into!

STRATEGIES FOR DEALING WITH FOOD AND NUTRITION

1. Use First/Then Sequences.

Use a visual to indicate taking one bite of a preferred food first, then a bite of a non-preferred food. Sometimes, the child needs to know that they can have their preferred food in between the other foods.

2. Take Slow, Steady Steps Forward.

Some children will struggle to even allow a new food to be on their plate, let alone put it in their mouths. Start with the new food sitting in a small bowl near their plate. Each day, move the bowl closer to their plate. Then put the bowl onto the plate. Then begin to slowly have them touch the new food with a spoon, or fork. Then touch the new food with their finger. Next, smell the new food for a few days. Keep increasing their interaction with the food, first putting it on their tongue and spitting it out, then putting it on their tongue and swallowing. This truly works—I promise!

3. Consult with a Physician, Dietician, or Nutritionist.

Talk to your physician and/or a nutritionist to ensure that the child is getting at least the minimal amount needed for physical health. Some health insurance plans will provide for nutritional support.

4. Stay Calm and Mellow.

Forcing children to eat when they are anxious or resistant will create a power struggle that is guaranteed to make mealtime a battlefield. Arguing with, cajoling, or punishing a child for not eating a particular food will create long-term emotional issues around food.

5. Eating Habits Change.

All of us change our eating habits throughout our lives. We may like a particular food for a while, then not eat it again for months. The goal is to ensure consistent, nutritional intake of a variety of foods. If that means that the child's diet consists of three vegetables, two fruits, one meat, and four dairy products, then that is fine. They may expand their eating repertoire when they get older. Or maybe not. But they are getting nutrition from all the food groups. It's a start.

6. Food is Food.

When you have a child who will eat only certain foods, flexibility is critical. If your child will eat chicken, carrots, and cheese sticks, then serve it for breakfast. If your child will eat yogurt, corn flakes, and grapes, then serve it for dinner. The concept that only certain foods can be eaten at certain times is cultural, not critical. The goal is a nutritious, varied diet, not that they eat breakfast foods at breakfast and dinner foods at dinner.

CHAPTER 4

Sounds of Silence: The Myth of Quiet

When our son Joshua was two years old, we were told that he had the "signs of a child with autism." We were sent to a child psychiatrist in our area who had supposedly done his internship in developmental disabilities and was an "expert in autism." This visit would change our lives forever.

Josh and I waited 45 minutes (an eternity!) in the waiting room of this doctor. The waiting room did not have toys, books, or anything remotely important and necessary to young children, even though the sign on his door read *Child* and Adolescent Psychiatry. When the doctor finally breezed into the waiting room, he told us to follow him into his office, and gee, sorry, he was a bit late. The room he led us to was literally his office—not a special place in which to see patients. There was an open candy bar on his desk, two chairs, a coffee table, lamps, and a wall of books—not a toy or play area in sight! He began our appointment by saying, "I haven't had time to read your file—why are you here?" I began to stumble and stammer through the words I had been given to describe Josh's behaviors, and the possibility that he might have autism. The doctor said, "Oh yes, Mrs. Beytien. He has autism and there are plenty of medications we can give him."

I spent the next ten minutes trying to keep Josh calm, and myself emotionally steady enough to ask coherent questions. As I babbled my way through questions and comments, this doctor finally held up his hand to me and said, "Mrs. Beytien! What is it you want from me?" I told him I wanted a diagnosis, a prescription for speech therapy, and a plan for how to help Joshua. He then uttered the following statement: "Mrs. Beytien, children like this never speak. Have you and your husband grieved over the loss of a child, and planned for his institution?"

In the days ahead, our efforts to grasp the finality of this doctor's statement left my husband and me as silent as our children. We were unable to comprehend the world we had been thrust into. Like our children, we could not seem to process all of the information that was coming at us. Everything seemed off-kilter. We struggled to understand how to act, speak, and behave in the world of silence and despair that this doctor conferred on us.

We grieved, we learned, and we struggled for a period of time. When clarity came, it thrust us into a very different world than the one that had been portrayed to us. Our autism world is loud: full of sounds, laughter, and movies playing non-stop! Our autism world has squeaked, grunted, and groaned its way into a life of joy, work, and constant commitment. There is no such thing as *silence* in an ABA therapy session!

Our home has been deafening at times with screams of frustration and words propelled by anxiety. The air has been punctuated by the off-key sounds of self-stimulation (repetitive body movements and sounds—also called "stimming"). The shouts, moans, screeches, scripting, and giggles are constant. And, surprisingly, we are grateful for each and every sound.

On most days, I can hear a variety of "autism sounds" in my home:

- Josh repeating his current favorite movie script while searching the internet and watching a DVD *all at the same time*!
- Zach, jumping up and down while watching *The Lion King,* screaming "Look Out!" and singing all of the songs; Zach, making our ceilings shake and light fixtures rattle
- The beep and clang of Spencer's GameCube, PlayStation, and computer games
- The slam of the bedroom door every morning when Zach heads for the bathroom
- The whir of the pizza cooker each morning as Zach makes his breakfast of Jack's Frozen Pepperoni Pizza, cut in half, then cubed when cooked
- The buzz and clank of innumerable trains running in the basement
- Josh's printer chugging away in the morning as it prints four pictures off the internet—ONLY four—not two or five, and all of this before his breakfast can be eaten

- The beep of the microwave each morning as Spencer fixes his breakfast of pancakes or waffles (every single morning!)
- The laughter of my husband as he continues to tease Spencer about dating girls

Self-stimulatory (stimming) behaviors can shift and change for individuals with autism. We saw changes in their sounds and movements as they reached puberty and we are seeing it shift and change as they move into adulthood. As a young child, Spencer would frequently bounce up and down when watching an exciting movie or video game. Joshua paced and bounced almost constantly when young, yet doesn't as a young adult. Joshua continues to slam his feet as he walks—we always know when he is coming down the stairs because you can hear the sound throughout the house! Zachary continues to jump and vocalize while watching his favorite movies, but for a shorter duration.

I often saw increases in self-stimulatory behaviors coincide with increases in language, social interaction, or academic knowledge. It appears that when their brains are firing off lots of neurons, their bodies can't stop moving and jerking!

Our first experience with this connection happened when Josh was in the 3rd grade. The first month of the new school year had gone smoothly and Josh appeared to be adjusting to his new teacher, new room, and new classmates rather well. Then we started to notice that his bouncing, rocking, and clenched-fist-in-front-of-my-crossed-eyes movement was significantly increasing. By the third month of school, the self-stimulatory behaviors were becoming disruptive to his class. Sensory processing activities were increased in his schedule, but there wasn't a reduction in the movement. I was concerned that he might have started having seizures, so I took him to a neurologist.

The neurologist requested an EEG. For seven days. No, "seven" is not a typographical error. Seven days. Seven days of electrodes on his head while connected to wires and a backpack with a monitor around his waist. Whenever possible, Josh was to be connected to a small computer tower instead of the battery-pack on his waist. I didn't think he would tolerate it or that the rest of the family would survive it! And he needed to go to school while wearing the electrodes and battery-pack.

We made the appointment and prepared for a week of upheaval. I did a presentation to his classmates about what was going to happen the week of the testing, and why Josh would be wearing a funny cap and backpack. I stocked up on his favorite things so that I could reward him for not ripping the electrodes off his head. This EEG was going to cost me almost as much in rewards as it was going to cost our medical insurance company!

At the neurologist's office, Josh did a great job handling the terrible smell of the "glue" that kept the electrodes on. He was excited about wearing a "computer" on his head. I had prepared for a battle and got a peace treaty instead. The process took nearly two hours and three bags of Skittles candy. Loaded with computer equipment, we got into our car and headed home.

As we exited the highway and made our way through our city, I stopped at a stoplight and checked my rearview mirror to see how Josh was handling the electrodes. As I looked at his reflection in my mirror, I saw him reach up to pull at the ponytail of electrical wires hanging down his back. I reflexively whipped around and said, "Josh!

Don't touch!"—and my foot slipped off the brake pedal. My car hit the back of the vehicle in front of me.

A Mercedes-Benz vehicle. From another state. Oh, dear.

I pulled over into a parking lot along with the Mercedes Benz. The stress of the prior three hours overwhelmed me, along with my frustration and horror at hitting another car, so I began to cry. Joshua is so curious about what has happened, that he has climbed into the front seat with me—wires, electrodes, computer and all. Imagine the scene that the other car's passengers found when they got out of their car at the parking lot. Crying woman on the phone, darling small boy with electrodes, wires and a variety of technical equipment piled into the front seat. They probably thought they weren't just in another state—they were in another dimension!

I got out of my car and tried to explain about Josh through my tears. I had phoned my mom to come get Joshua, the police department to report the accident, and phoned my husband to come get me! The other passengers were exceptionally kind. They were visiting grandchildren in our city. We eventually got all the car accident information, reports written, and personal information exchanged. And I went home to start a week of this situation. (By the way, I found out weeks later that the other passengers wouldn't let our insurance pay for any of their damage. They sent a note to me saying that they were capable of taking care of their car, and I should focus on taking care of my son. The kindness of strangers can be astonishing.)

The week of the EEG went fine, and Joshua did not have any seizures. He was completely comfortable with the electrodes, and seemed to revel in unplugging himself from his computer tower and walking around with the backpack. I think he just enjoyed the attention and the continuing influx of Thomas the Tank engine rewards! So although he didn't have any seizures, which was good, I was still puzzled by the massive amount of self-stim that he was exhibiting.

The self-stim behaviors decreased drastically about a month after the EEG. And his skill levels increased drastically right after that period. More extensive language, increased academic ability, increased appropriate social engagement with classmates and family. It seemed as if his brain was working so hard to create new learning pathways, that his body couldn't stop moving in response. This pattern has been true for his whole life. And it has been true for Zachary, and many of the individuals that I work with. There are periods of increased sound, movement, and self-stimulatory behaviors prior to increased skill levels. I don't have any research to prove this connection, just observation. But knowing this helps me to keep the changing stimulatory behaviors in perspective.

If the stimulatory behaviors occur in public, I respond to the situation that is occurring. For example, if Joshua is flapping his arms a bit while waiting in line at the grocery store, I'll ask him what he is thinking about. He typically stops and tells me what was on his mind. If Zach is jumping and pacing while at the park, I will give him a visual picture of an activity to choose, or have him play catch with me to occupy himself. I have observed increases in stimulatory behavior when the person with autism isn't actively engaged in learning or some other activity. So my response is to give the person something to do, or something to discuss with me.

I also have my humorous response to autism movements. Many times, when Josh or Zach is making some unusual body movements

out in public, I begin to dance right next to them. I can dance relatively well and their movements look like some new, trendy dance
routine! So I "dance" along beside them, giving the people who are
staring at the boys a context for the movement. I might even say, "It's a
family thing" in response to the look of puzzlement on people's faces.
Of course, my husband will tell me to stop dancing, and Spencer may
walk down a different aisle in the store because he's embarrassed, but
I'm having a good time!

The sounds of autism are joyous, and frustrating, and memorable,
and illuminating, and critically important in our lives. These sounds
let us know that life is moving forward, that the boys are progress-
ing, living, and enjoying their lives. I am immeasurably glad that "Dr.
Doomsayer" was unbelievably wrong. We did not "lose" our children.
We found ourselves instead.

Okay. I'll confess. My favorite sound is silence, but *only* if it means
that the boys are blissfully sleeping!

Strategies for Dealing with Self-Stimulatory Behavior ("Stimming")

1. Shape, Don't Eliminate, Self-stimulatory Behaviors.

The movements of autism are part of the diagnosis. Insisting
that the person with autism cannot flap his hands or bounce
will usually result in an escalation of behaviors that are more
difficult to deal with than the self-stimulatory behaviors.

Instead, shape the behavior by evaluating the purpose of the movement, and giving the person something to replace it. If the person is flapping their hands, give them a stress ball to move back and forth between their hands. If the person needs to pace, give them a visual schedule and visual structure of when, where, and how long they can pace. Replace chewing on clothing with chewing on a toothbrush or gum.

2. Exercise.

Ensuring that the person has sufficient exercise every day will reduce self-stimulatory behaviors. Many of the stimulatory behaviors can be translated to physical activities such as long-distance running, cross-country skiing, speed-walking or running hurdles. Be creative! One young man I worked with needed to pace frequently, and would refuse to work if he couldn't pace. In order to give him the movement he needed, yet still get his work done, I separated his work tasks and put some of the tasks at one end of a hallway, and the rest at the other end of the hallway. His visual schedule was changed to indicate "work, walk, work" and we showed him how to follow the schedule. His work productivity increased, and his challenging behaviors decreased.

3. Eliminate "Downtime."

There is a significant amount of time in educational settings and at home, when the person with autism is "waiting" for the next activity. This time period, "downtime," without mental or physical engagement, leaves the person with autism without direction. Self-stimulatory behavior, verbal scripting, or other inappropriate behaviors occur most frequently at this time. Eliminating the amount of "downtime" in their day will also reduce stimulatory behaviors. Make their day purposeful and engaging.

CHAPTER 5

On Any Given Day: Challenging Behavior

"Some days I wonder how my kids will turn out, but most days I'm figuring out how to survive them right now."

—BRIAN ANDREAS (Artist and Author)

A gentleman approached me after a workshop I had given in Illinois. He complimented me profusely on how practical the information that I had presented was to him, and told me that he and his wife had also attended a presentation I had given a year earlier. He proceeded to tell me that my insights into my boys' autism had made a huge impact on his family, and that whenever they were having a really difficult time with their son, they thought of me. I was feeling rather wonderful at this moment, and very proud of my work. This loving father then said, "Yes, every time our lives seem rather difficult, my wife and I say to each other, "Well, at least we're not Alyson!"

That gave me pause. I never intended to serve as the "misery standard" against which other parents of children with autism would compare their lot in life! And, I certainly don't think of my life as miserable—in fact, quite the opposite (at least on most days). I know that my life can be more intense than that of others—and more stressful, and more hectic, and more worrisome. Okay, maybe I'm kidding myself. My life is probably more *EVERYTHING* than those of most other people on the planet!

Admittedly, like Alexander (in the popular children's book), we've certainly had our share of "terrible, horrible, no-good, very bad days." Our boys have had quite a list of challenging behaviors. On any given day (week, month, year) we have dealt with the following unusual behaviors and challenges:

- Licking cement
- Shattering glass objects (just to hear the sound)
- Watching toys spin in a flushing toilet (resulting in the replacement of four toilets in a month)
- Insisting on wearing only certain clothing
- Turning all of the lights on and off, and on and off, and on and off (You get the idea!)
- Insisting that you drive the same route to school every single day
- Taking clothes off everywhere (and anywhere)
- Watching the same video 3,000 times—in one day (or so it seems)
- Leaving the house in the middle of the night
- Humming like an electric motor

- Chewing on clothing, sand, plants, and other inedibles
- Biting, kicking, hitting, hair pulling, head-banging, etc.
- Shredding clothing and shoes with bare hands
- Darting into the street or parking lot

We've learned that some behaviors fade by themselves, but that others take a significant amount of intervention. Some behaviors make you laugh, while others make you cry. Some days we work on eliminating a particularly challenging behavior, only to have it replaced by a behavior that is much worse.

The particularly difficult days stand out in my mind, like the time I found Spencer pouring laundry detergent all over his room; or the day when Zach got into the locked cabinet of cleaners and poured bleach all over the new living room carpet; or the time Zachary stripped naked in the middle of the playland at Burger King; or the day Josh cut all of the wires to his computer while it was plugged in. I also remember when Joshua went through a "mad scientist" period and every time he wasn't being supervised, he pulled all of the spices and other similar ingredients out of the kitchen cabinets so that he could pour them into a bowl of water for a "potion." Come to think of it, Zachary had a "Houdini" period when he was able to escape every car seat, locked door, and bolted window that we had!

There is one episode, however, that is forever etched into my memory. At the time this occurred, we were living next to an empty lot that had a monstrous pile of dirt, a remnant from a newly-dug basement foundation. On this particular day, I was filling the bathtub for three-year-old Zach (for the fifth time that day) when

I looked out the bathroom window and spotted our dog running over the top of the dirt pile. The dog had jumped our fence, and was happily cavorting through the mud and rain. I turned off the bath water, quickly took Zach back to his room to watch a movie, and went downstairs to get the dog. I realized that if I went out the front door, Spencer and Joshua might hear it and follow me outside. So, I bolted the front door, and went out the back door, into the rain, through the gate, and around the front of the house to get to the dog. As I chased the dog over some dead branches and through the mud, it did occur to me that perhaps I should have worn shoes. Sure enough—I stepped on a branch of thorns, and embedded five huge ones in the bottom of my foot. Somehow, I did manage to collar the dog.

I dragged the dog around to the gate, only to find four-year-old Joshua, crying and screaming for me outside the gate. He had figured out my backdoor ruse and followed me outside. *He had also shut the back door behind him, which caused it to automatically lock.* So, there I was, standing outside in the pouring rain with five thorns in my foot, a screaming child by my side, and a renegade dog! I can only imagine what the scene would look like to others—thank heaven the lot next door was empty! The task—not an easy one under the circumstances—was to get back into the house where my other two children were, hopefully, still watching a movie.

Desperate, I discovered a window in my garage that was slightly open. I broke the screen, and tried to lift Joshua into the window so that he could open the door. Josh, however, was not willing to cooperate at this point (being rather traumatized by the rain, and unusual events of the day). At that point, I threw the dog into the backyard, and proceeded to haul myself through the window, injured foot and all, with Josh in tow.

It was at this point, that I heard water—*inside the house*—and I realized that it wasn't rain! I hobbled as quickly as I could up the stairs, only to see water pouring out of my bathroom. Zachary had obviously been upset by not getting to have his bath, so he had figured out how to turn the water on in the tub, and water had been running ever since I ran out of the house to rescue the dog. There was water everywhere. I frantically tried to soak up the water before it ruined the carpet and wood floors. I heard the back door open, and started to yell "NO!" to Spencer, who had just let the muddy dog inside the house. I tried to run back down the stairs to save the living room carpet, but tripped over the wet towels, falling on my face and my now throbbing foot.

Inexplicably, I did make it downstairs, got the dog back outside, and picked up the phone to call my husband, Craig. At that moment, Spencer turned the corner of the kitchen, and I saw his five-year-old face decorated like an Indian warrior with *permanent* marker.

Don't worry. The story has a happy ending. Craig came home from work (does the expression *reinforcements have arrived* come to mind?), and after the shock wore off, he helped get everyone and everything clean and back in order. And, of course, the day did eventually end.

I have read that the formula for comedy is "tragedy plus time." I think that's really true. The crisis of today is the humor of tomorrow, if we will just recognize that struggles are part and parcel of life and that, at some point, the crisis will pass. As parents of children with autism, we may have a larger portion of struggles than others. Our lives with our kids who have autism are MORE everything—more difficult, funny, loving, zany, intense, and unusual. All things considered, I think that's a good thing. It makes us MORE everything as humans and as parents.

But on any given day, I might just want it to be a little LESS!

STRATEGIES FOR DEALING WITH BEHAVIOR CHALLENGES

1. Have a Stress Strategy.

Whether it is deep breathing, singing a song, cursing in your mind, or repeating "There's no place like home" over and over again, you need a plan for keeping yourself calm when everything is falling apart. Choose what works for you. Then practice, practice, practice.

2. Think Low and Slow.

When you feel yourself getting ready to yell or raise your voice, think Low and Slow. Lower your voice tone, and slow down your words. When upset, our voices tend to get higher in pitch and faster in speed, which typically escalates the child's behavior also. Raising your voice will raise their anxiety. So drop your tone to bass and slow it down to a turtle speed.

3. Write a Behavior Plan.

Writing down a specific response for a specific behavior helps solidify how to react when the challenging moments happen.

For example, if your child falls to the ground screaming every time you walk down the cereal aisle in the grocery store, then decide how you will respond and write it down. Just like the visual schedule you show your child before entering the store, you review your own plan before the moment arrives.

4. Reward Yourself and Your Child.

Rewards are a critical part of changing behavior. This is true for your child and for you! So determine what your reward will be for handling a difficult moment with restraint and aplomb.

CHAPTER 6

Disney DNA: Echolalia and Language Challenges

There is general consensus by researchers that there is a genetic basis to autism—at least in some cases. The exact number of genes affected, how they are affected, which genes cause impairments in language versus social understanding, and a plethora of other questions are still being studied by a host of researchers in countries around the world. If we could pinpoint the genetic foundation and triggers for autism we would likely move forward toward treatment, prevention, and cure.

Having three sons with an autism spectrum disorder, a nephew with Asperger's syndrome, and a deceased uncle who probably had autism ensures that our family is the geneticists' idea of "winning the lottery"! We have participated in a number of genetic research studies, and were one of the first 100 families to donate our blood to the

Autism Genetic Resource Exchange (AGRE). We did this through Cure Autism Now (CAN) almost 12 years ago. We've been part of research projects at the University of Chicago, the University of North Carolina, Chapel Hill, and many other centers. Although my boys aren't big fans of having their blood drawn, we have felt compelled to offer what little help we can in determining the causes of autism. A small amount of our time and a prick of the needle are worth it in the long run, if it helps researchers to find answers.

I am not a doctor, so my understanding of chromosomes, genetic mutations, and other pieces of genetic research is rather limited. I am, however, involved on a daily basis in the outward expression of autism, and with various interventions, even if I am not privy to the inner workings of this puzzling condition. That said, I have done some of my own observational research into autism, and I have come to the conclusion that there is a single "gene" consistent in nearly 99% of individuals with autism. I call it the *Disney gene*.

Every parent out there can pinpoint this gene in his or her child. Doubtful? See if this sounds familiar: At an early age, the child will watch ONLY Disney movies. Some children narrow their focus to the Disney Princess movies, while others attach themselves to the old versions of *Bambi* (and definitely NOT the new ones!). Still others can recite whole dialogues from a variety of Disney movies. But ONLY Disney movies. Yes, I know there is the *Thomas the Tank Engine* gene (apparent in two of my own sons, and clearly a "genetic player" in autism!), but the Disney gene seems to have the edge, crossing gender, age, and railroad barriers. It's as if there is a Disney DNA strand imbedded into autism.

The ability to recite Disney dialogues has provided many hilarious moments in our lives. Our Zachary is the most fluent in Disney talk. My favorite Disney moment of Zach's occurred when he was six years old. He was essentially non-verbal, despite his "bouts" of Disney echolalia. (Echolalia is the immediate or delayed repetition of the exact words spoken by others.) We had some friends and their kids over to visit and to "play" (even though *play* was a difficult concept for Zach and my other sons at that time, and a concept almost beyond their abilities). Surprisingly, the interaction had gone fairly well, and as our guests were piling into their cars to leave, I decided that it was a good time to have the boys practice the skill of saying goodbye. So I took them onto the porch, and prompted them to say *goodbye* and wave. Zachary was doing his "Tigger" bounce on the porch and flapping his hands. All of a sudden, he clearly yells out to our friends, "IF YOU EVER COME BACK WE'LL KILL YOU!"

Can you name that Disney movie? Think about it. It's *The Lion King*. In the movie Simba leaves, and the hyenas stand on a cliff and yell, "If you ever come back, we'll KILL you!" I was struck by Zachary's clever association. He is thinking, "Wait—I'm standing on the porch; people are leaving; my mom wants me to say something." Bingo! He recites the departure line from his favorite Disney movie as our company is departing. The words are completely appropriate to the situation in his mind, even though—absent knowledge of *The Lion King*, the brilliance (yes, *brilliance!*) of the association is lost.

A few months ago, while consulting in an elementary school, I saw a young student working on identifying pictures of boys versus girls. When handed a picture of a boy or man, the child would say, "I want to be a real boy!" in perfect imitation of Pinocchio. When shown a picture of a girl or woman, he would indicate his knowledge by singing perfectly on pitch, "Come on, and, kiss the girl," just like the cranky crustacean in *The Little Mermaid* did. I thought it was hilarious, not to mention brilliant. After all, he did get the answers right!

The Disney gene has made its presence known in many situations that have come up over the years. I've written some of the best Disney "one liners" below. See if you can guess the Disney movie they come from. One of the lines isn't from a Disney movie, but close enough! (Answers are below.)

- Anytime Zach is eating something and we ask him if he wants ketchup, or mustard, or butter, or syrup, he says, "MUSTARD!! Mustard? No, no, no, no. Butter? Now that's another thing entirely."
- If we ask Zach to come downstairs to eat a meal, he yells from upstairs, "Then go ahead and STAAARRRVE! If she doesn't eat with me, she doesn't eat at all!"
- For a period of about two years, if my husband spoke to Zach, Zachary would respond with "Dad! You're scaring people!"
- When Zach is agitated or angry, he yells "Dead Broad off the Table!"
- If Zachary gets new clothing or shoes, and someone comments on his clothes, he responds with "Why Lady! You got a new collar."
- If you give Zach a kiss, he shuffles his feet, grins sheepishly, and says, "Oh, garsh!"

I have found myself quoting Disney movies sometimes, probably because I have watched them so frequently and because I spend most of my days around individuals with autism. What I forget is that other people don't always know that I'm quoting a movie. I was in a meeting the other day, with some very important people. I was given a compliment on some work I had done, and without thinking of how it would sound, I said, "There is no charge for Awesomeness. Or Attractiveness." This is one of my favorite lines from the movie, *Kung Fu Panda.* But saying it out loud, without the reference point, caused everyone to look at me rather oddly. When I realized what I had done, I apologized and said, "It's an autism thing." Most people around the table just nodded their head and slowly turned away.

Zachary and my other two boys have the ability to say these lines with the exact tone and facial expressions of the characters. The general public is not as adept at remembering and quoting these Disney favorites, so I find myself having to explain what I find so hilarious. Nor do people generally realize that there are some really awful things said in Disney movies, until one of my kids yells "Quiet, you great Clooney!" or "Shut up, you idiot!" when someone is too loud. Since it's difficult to explain the whole language / echolalia / social understanding piece, I just say, "It's genetic!" Then I smile and walk away.

Answers to the Disney Movie Trivia: 1) The Mad Hatter in *Alice in Wonderland*; 2) the beast in *Beauty and the Beast*; 3) Max says it to Goofy in *The Goofy Movie;* 4) Shrek in *Shrek*; 5) The bloodhound in *Lady and the Tramp*; and, 6) Bashful in *Snow White and the Seven Dwarfs.*

STRATEGIES FOR DEALING WITH ECHOLALIA

1. Echolalia and Delayed Echolalia Can Be Used to Teach Appropriate Language.

When a child with autism can repeat a movie script in the appropriate situation, they are demonstrating emotional under-standing of the situation and the generalization of language. This is great! Immediately model the appropriate phrase back to them. Practice using the appropriate words, not the scripted phrase, whenever possible.

2. Let Others Know What Movies Are Being Scripted.

Tell everyone involved with the child what current movie scripts are being used and how to respond. Consistent modeling of appropriate language is critical to changing the scripts to spon-taneous verbal language.

3. Teach Flexibility.

Individuals with ASD need to learn flexibility. If a child is fixated on a particular movie, then use a visual schedule to show them how to choose other movies. For example; put six pictures of their favorite movie on a choice card, along with one picture of a different, but favorite, movie. They can choose which movie to watch from the choice card. After they choose all six pictures of the current favored movie, there is only the picture of the other movie available. They may not watch their favorite movie until they watch at least some portion of the second favorite. Continue to expand choices until they can choose from a variety of movies without anxiety.

4. Laugh. It Really Is Funny!

Writing down what your child says will provide you with hours of entertainment in later years. Trust me!

CHAPTER 7

Refusing Puberty: Adolescence and Sexuality

C AUTION: The following article, written several years ago, contains an explicit discussion of adolescent issues, and may cause severe heart palpitations in parents of young children with autism!☺

I am in trouble—serious, deep trouble! I've read books on adolescence; gone to workshops on relationships and sexuality, taught my boys the information they need to know about adolescence and the terms they need to learn. But I'm still in trouble. I've known it since Josh was eight years old and we had "The Mermaid Incident."

I was walking past the downstairs bathroom one day when Joshua was eight. The bathroom door was open (they hadn't yet grasped the concept of privacy), and I saw Josh sitting on the toilet, pants at his ankles, studying a *Victoria's Secret* catalog with great intensity. (No comment on where that came from!) I asked him what he was doing. "Looking at mermaids, Mom," replied Josh. Needless to say, the catalog was "lost" and the subscription cancelled!

A few months later, I went down to our basement and saw Joshua lying on the couch with his hand down his pants. Josh heard me coming, and whipped his hand out. I asked him, "Josh, what are you doing?" He responded, quite agitatedly, "I'M THINKING!" (I am NOT going to comment on how appropriate that statement may or may not be for the male gender!) I then asked him, "What are you thinking about?" He said, "Mermaids."

That's when I knew that puberty was going to be beyond my degree in Early Childhood Special Education!

Fast-forward a few years:

Joshua is handsome, funny, quirky, loving, and affectionate, and has always been the darling of the girls in his classroom. While that was fine when he was eight and thinking of girls as mermaids, it has challenging ramifications now that he is 12 years old and thinking of girls as, well, *girls*.

As his mother, I want to refuse puberty. Can I do that? Pleeease! Dating? Are you kidding? The thought of my boys kissing girls is overwhelming enough, but I worry about whether they will be able to understand the emotions that go with it. And then there is that *other* thing. I didn't want to know about masturbation when my brothers told me about it in high school. So you can imagine how I feel about having to teach my guys when and where to do it. (And I thought getting them to understand how to pee in the toilet was difficult!)

The funny thing about it is, you never know when the SUBJECT is about to come up. Just a few nights ago my parents, the boys, and I were sitting at the dinner table. It was actually a quiet meal—everyone was eating and reading, silent in his or her own thoughts. Out of the silence, Josh turned to me and stated, matter-of-factly, "Mom, I don't want hair on my penis."

Now, I'm rarely at a loss for words, but this had me frantically commanding my face not to react, and my mouth to keep shut. Meanwhile, my parents were sputtering in laughter and trying to hide it. Mustering up a surrealistically calm façade, I asked Josh, "Honey, what made you think of that?"

"Well, Spencer does and I don't want it," he replied, completely unaware that this "dinner conversation" might be better saved for another time and place, AND that his brother might not want him sharing this intimate information with other people. So, now what do I say? (And did I even want to know that my other son has "it.")

"Josh, sweetheart, I can't change the fact that you are growing up. You get hair on your penis when you get older."

"But I don't want it! You're in charge of the schedule—change it!"

And therein lies the challenge. I've told them for years that I'm in charge of the schedule. Surprise, surprise, Josh took me literally! But, I'm not in charge of puberty, because if I were in charge, it would be a vastly different process! What I can be in charge of, however, is their knowledge about puberty and about the changes that go along with it. So we have structured discussions on a consistent basis about growing up. I have books with pictures, and I try to remain calm and informative when the inevitable challenging questions come up.

We have also learned that adolescence brings with it changes in the social skills that we have taught the boys for most of their lives. In our house, "shut up," "stupid," and "idiot" are "curse" words, along with the actual ones. So when the boys were getting ready to go to junior high school, I knew we would have to discuss the fact that other kids could say those words and not get into trouble. I sat our oldest son down one evening and began to lay out the social story for the shifting rules that make junior high school such a difficult place for many young people with ASD. I explained to him that there were some words that kids would *not* get in trouble for saying, and some words that they *would* get in trouble for saying. He asked me what words would get him in trouble. I began to list the inappropriate curse words that junior high kids use. Mentally, I was gearing myself up for the dreaded "F" word (which, by the way, I can honestly say I had never previously uttered). Prior to telling my guy this word, I told him that it was the ultimate horrible word, that everyone in society knows that it is a horrible, ugly word, and that everyone gets into trouble for saying it, because it is so very awful. And then ... I said it! Spencer looked at me for a moment, soundlessly mouthed the word, and then said to me with a puzzled look on his face, "But Mom, it's only one syllable. That doesn't sound that bad." I think he was expecting something like *supercalifragilisticexpialadocious*!

And so it goes. The school year has begun, and we are finding out that there are more rules in junior high that we haven't discussed, but need to teach. Josh is still my ladies' man, saying hello to all the girls. Spencer has grown eight inches, is growing a moustache, and will not hug me at school anymore. (As hard as that is, that's a good thing.) And I am still wondering if I know how to handle the oncoming years. I do know that the shifting sands of the social landscape will cause us to stumble and fall a few times. I just want to keep the stumbling to a minimum, and get the boys through the next few years with their self esteem intact, which means that I will continue to teach them and discuss with them what is appropriate and what is not.

We had one of our talks just the other night. Spencer, Josh, and I were looking through the picture books and rehearsing the terminology to use when discussing issues related to puberty. As I have learned—sometimes painfully—to leave nothing to chance, I also made the boys aware of the people that they could and could not discuss these things with. Just as I was about to turn the page, Josh looked at me and said, in his most disgruntled "teenage" voice, "I feel a moral coming on!" I laughed out loud as I sent them to bed! After that incident, I made a decision. I REFUSE TO DISCUSS PUBERTY FOR AT LEAST ANOTHER THREE DAYS!

STRATEGIES FOR DEALING WITH PUBERTY

1. Developmental Delay Does Not Mean Physical Delay.

Puberty will arrive whether you or your child is ready. Chronological age determines puberty, not emotional age. Most children are discussing issues around sexuality by age nine or ten. The average age for the onset of menstruation is ten. At this age, your child will at least need to know the basic terms of the body and sexuality so that they can know which words they should repeat and which ones they shouldn't.

2. Teach the Concept of Public versus Private.

Using the words "public" and "private" to describe the concepts of sexuality will allow everyone to be clear about expected behavior. Everything can be divided into these two categories: there are topics that are public versus private, body parts that are public or private, people who are public or private, etc. If your teenager launches into a discussion of breasts in the middle of the grocery store, you can defer the topic for later by saying, "That's a private topic. This is a public place. We need to discuss that in a private place."

3. Determine Your Family Values and Rules Regarding Sexual Relationships.

When will you allow your child to date? Can they have sex before marriage? You will need to be clear about your rules, and teach them early. Obviously, no parent can guarantee that a child will adopt their values. But individuals with ASD need some rules and boundaries to keep them safe.

4. Honor "No."

One of the biggest worries many parents face is ensuring that their child with autism is safe from abuse. Even individuals with autism spectrum disorder can misinterpret intent and be taken advantage of. Sometimes this happens because the person has been taught to be "compliant" without being allowed to say "no." We should respect, and honor, the right to say "no" with every person. If we teach how to say "no" appropriately, then we can also teach how to say "no" to a potential abuser.

5. Wanting a Relationship with Another Person Is Human.

Remember that all individuals want to feel a connection to other people. If we don't teach the appropriate way to make those connections, individuals with autism will find another way—and we probably won't like it! If a teenager with autism is behaving inappropriately with a girl he likes, then teach him the right way to let a girl know he likes her. And if an individual with autism isn't given any opportunity to create connective relationships, aggressive and inappropriate behavior will escalate.

CHAPTER 8

The Weatherman: Mood Shifts

I love the weather channel. My husband and I watch it every morning as we get ready for the day. Growing up as "valley girls" in Southern California, my friends and I used to make jokes about the local weathermen: "Weathermen in Los Angeles don't need a degree in meteorology, just a sense of humor!" The weather is constant in Southern California— 72° and partly sunny. I've lived in the Midwest for over 15 years now, and actually love the changing seasons. I've learned to adjust, and appreciate the good weather and the bad.

My personal weatherman is our youngest son, Zachary. I can tell the climate of our day within 15 minutes of his waking up. If he crawls into bed with me and grins, it will likely be sunny and clear, with possible language. If he comes into my room and growls at me with an angry face, it will undoubtedly be cloudy and unsteady with possible hitting. If he screams or yells within the first 15 minutes of the day, watch out for thunderstorms with potentially damaging winds. And if he awakens me by hitting me, sound the WINTER STORM WARNING. BLIZZARD APPROACHING!

I'm frequently baffled by the intermittent fluctuations in Zachary's moods. There are, however, whole seasons of "bad weather," and those can be difficult to endure. February and March can be as miserable inside our house as it can be outside. We try to accommodate and adjust for the climactic shifts. I will add in more visual systems, sensory input, change my boys' diets, and create new motivating behavior management plans. We look for the typical factors that affect other people adversely such as the holiday letdown and the winter blahs. But mostly, we hold on until spring!

The other day I found myself weathering a day of storms. Zach was edgy, angry, and aggressive, and so was I! (Well, I was at least two out of the three.) He and I had just worked through a "winter squall" that had come out of nowhere—at least it had seemed so to me. I walked away from him, only to feel him coming up behind me. I braced myself, and waited to be hit or kicked. Instead, I got a hug, a kiss on my cheek, and a "Sorry. Be nice." Oh my—the eye of the storm! I stood still, in awe and amazement over the language (he's basically non-verbal) and marveled at the climactic shift from emotional to calm. I knew we would have another outburst soon, but I have learned to appreciate those small moments of sunshine no matter what their duration or frequency.

It's amazing how Zach's daily emotional weather fluctuations affect the whole household, especially me. An example: If Zach starts his day yelling and screaming, that upsets Josh, who likes total quiet in the morning. So they start escalating in their yelling and anger. Then Dad gets involved, in an attempt to moderate the stormy conditions. That's when the emotional tempest rises to a Class One storm. Like cascading bolts of lightning, Josh will yell at Spencer over something so that Spencer gets frustrated with him. Then Zach will hit Josh in defense of Spencer (his hero). Josh is then likely to throw a train at Zach, who then runs to Grandma for support, while everyone else runs to me to make the storm go away. Our Class One storm has just escalated to a Class Two, and it's only 7:00 in the morning!

Moms are notorious for trying to make everyone happy and for doing everything they can to calm the storms of life. Yet, I've realized that I have only a small amount of control over Zach's internal state, just as I have minimal control over the weather outside. But I can live, and learn, in each season. And I can surely appreciate the days of spring, having just lived through winter.

Winter can be difficult for individuals with autism. My phone starts to ring incessantly with requests for consultation about the second week of January. For the majority of the U.S., January is cold, snowy, wet, and miserable. While I don't have multiple-subject research to support my theory, I think that winter is difficult for three reasons: 1) the children cannot get outside and move as much as they are used to 2) they have sensory overload with the many layers of clothing that we are constantly putting on and taking off, and 3) they experience a type of Seasonal Affective Disorder (S.A.D.) with the depletion of sunshine.

STRATEGIES FOR DEALING
WITH "STORMY WEATHER"

1. Increase Exercise When the Mood Swings Begin.

Exercise increases the positive endorphins that our brain needs to remain calm and cheerful. My general rule is to ensure that a person with autism has at least three 20-minute sessions of cardio exercise every day. This can be combined into two 30-minute sessions, or any other combination that works for the person. Exercise will significantly reduce physical aggression and increase mood stability.

2. Medication Is an Option, but Should Be the Last Resort.

The first response to mood swings and increased challenging behaviors is to evaluate the data and attempt to pinpoint the cycles. Ensure that visual schedules make sense and are being used, that sensory challenges are moderated with therapy, and that the person has the ability to communicate his or her needs in some manner. If those critical needs are being met, but the problems remain, then consultation with your physician should include discussion of medication for stabilization of mood.

3. Increase Choice-making throughout the Day.

Review the visual schedules to ensure that there are many opportunities for individuals to make choices and be in control of their lives. Everything has a choice. Taking a shower may not be a choice—but when you take the shower, what soap you use, what shampoo you use, or whether you brush your teeth before or after the shower are all choices that can be made. The more choices people have, the happier they are.

4. Create and Teach a Relaxation Routine.

Teaching a person with challenging behavior and emotional cycles how to relax is a lifelong skill. Create a short, clear relaxation routine that can be done anywhere the "meltdown" might happen. This could be a series of breathing exercises, hand presses, counting, or scripting. The routine needs to be taught in the calm, happy moments, with visual supports that will eventually be the cues needed in the challenging moment.

CHAPTER 9

The Love Language of Autism: Expressing Affection

I read a book by Gary Chapman entitled *The Five Love Languages*. The premise of the book is that all of us "speak" and understand love in different ways. I read this book in my quest to better support and communicate with my husband because, although I adore him, I don't always seem to speak his love language. Now I know that sounds odd, but the premise does have some validity.

Mr. Chapman believes that there are five ways to understand love. We understand it through *quality time, words of affirmation, physical touch, acts of service,* and *receiving gifts*. He believes that we often show our love in the way that we want to have love shown to us. And although the book is written for couples, the last chapter examines the same theory as applied to children.

So I thought about my boys, and contemplated how they might understand love. This can be an interesting exercise when one considers that many professionals believe that individuals with autism don't understand love as we do, or that they are incapable of taking another person's point of view sufficiently to even understand love. Have you ever asked yourself if your children understand love, or if they know that you love them?

I can tell you that my son Spencer understands love by physical touch. He likes us to throw our arms around his shoulders, give him a discreet hug before he goes to school each morning, and sit as close as possible to him on the couch when we watch movies together. Joshua understands love by "tokens of affection." So, if I buy him something—big or small—every day, he feels cheerful and loved. He actually gives me lists of things to buy him on a frequent basis! A mere trip to the gas station for a Nerds rope candy will have him expressing affection and undying devotion to me. (Too bad everyone in my life isn't this easy to please!)

Then I started thinking about my son Zachary, and I was at a loss to figure out his love language. I contemplated this for days, and nothing really fit. Then it hit me. Zachary speaks in the love language of autism. There is actually a *sixth* language that author Gary Chapman doesn't even know about!

Zach speaks his love language by backing into us for a hug (because facing us is too difficult for him). Zach speaks his love language by wiping off the kisses we give him with the back of his hand, and by crawling into our bed each morning and saying "Hi Mama." Zach's love language includes wrapping his arms around my neck and yanking my head toward his for a really, really close-up "hello."

Zach also speaks his love by jumping up and down and making high pitched cheerful sounds, by showing us his dimple when he smiles, and by constantly speaking our names to get our attention.

Zachary knows he's loved because I know to buy him ONLY Jack's Frozen Pepperoni Pizza. He knows he's loved because I can sing all of the songs from *The Lion King* by heart, along with him. Zach also knows that his parents love him because we understand that Dr. Seuss is one of the greatest authors ever, that a family vacation *must* include water, and that tooth brushing is painful.

Children with autism can have so many different (and unconventional) ways of expressing their love. And yes, there are days and times when I wonder if our boys truly understand how deeply their father and I love them. During the first days of diagnosis and subsequent emotional upheaval, my husband and I decided that we had two really important goals for our guys. One was that they would know without doubt that they are loved, and two, that they would have joy in their lives. Anything else would be icing on the cake. With those lifelong goals in mind, we have had IEP goals for years that focus on learning how to be a good friend, and on teaching the boys how to understand friendship and love.

That said, sometimes I worry that the tremendous focus on teaching social skills to our children, and on promoting interactions is not so much a matter of trying to fulfill *their* needs, as it is our attempt to change their love language. If our children are happy with only one or two friends, and if they spend hours sitting next to someone playing video games, never speaking more than two sentences to each other—who are we to say that their friendship isn't valid?

I still work on ensuring that my boys know that they are loved—

deeply, honestly, eternally loved. I demonstrate this by acknowledging each one of my sons' personal love language, and by trying to speak it back to him so that each one can feel my love in the "language" that he understands. Sometimes I am successful, and sometimes, I fail miserably. But I do keep trying.

One day, I was full of angst and "mother guilt." Zach and I had tried to go to the park with a group of typical peers, and the outing had not gone well (you know—tantrums, hitting, screaming, no interaction!). I drove home obsessing over what I had done wrong (*"Why did I think we could do this?"*), what I had not done (*"Why didn't I take pictures of the playground ahead of time and prepare him?"*), and generally increasing my anxiety level every second of the drive home. I finally couldn't take it any longer, and pulled the car over next to a lake by our house. Zach loves to throw rocks into water, so he cheerfully climbed out of the car. I was still so caught up in my self-flagellation that I didn't pay attention to where he went. When I finally noticed him, he was on the other side of the lake. Just as I was getting ready to go and get him, he looked at me across the lake. It was a moment of searing eye contact. Then Zach raised his hand, and waved at me. He had never done that before! When I waved back, he began to run around the edge of the lake, toward me, with his arms outstretched. That is a moment I will never forget. Because I knew with great clarity, right then, that he LOVED me, and he knew that his love was reciprocated.

The love language of autism is often complicated and difficult to understand. But I know that it exists. And I would guess that each of you could list the ways in which your children speak and understand love. I also know that even though our lists would differ, they would still speak the love language of autism—deep and abiding, long-suffering and exquisite, truer and more immeasurable than anything we had ever thought we could feel for another human being.

LOVE STRATEGIES?

How do I approach "strategies for loving your child"? To suggest that, somehow, you *don't* know how to love your child would be arrogant, and against my belief that parents love their children unconditionally. There are times when I hear physicians, clinicians, and educational professionals express their frustration at a particularly intense parent. When possible, I quietly remind everyone that the parent/child relationship is inherently protective and intense. It's the "mother bear" protecting her cub. As parents, we will instinctively defend our child, even if it appears irrational or out of proportion.

I have had many parents relate to me the moment that a physician or other professional gave them a diagnosis of autism for their child. For one family, the physician said, "Yes, your child has autism. You're just going to have to learn to love him." I was appalled at the arrogance and assumption that this family would have to be taught to love their child.

Oftentimes, the challenge is to help those outside our family see what we as parents see. In my experience, parents don't need lessons or strategies on how to love their children. It's innate, involuntary and constant—like breathing.

CHAPTER 10

Confessions of a Gecko Killer: Teaching Death and Loss

My 12-year-old budding herpetologist was devastated. His prized albino leopard gecko was dead—in a newly cleaned aquarium sitting on the back patio on a sunshiny day. The "best Christmas present ever" lay shriveled up on top of his water dish, eyes blackened and nearly smoking. And it was my fault.

I didn't mean to kill the lizard. I thought it would be a good idea to clean his aquarium while it was warm enough outside to not need his heat lamp. I found out it was warm enough to fry a gecko through the glass walls of the aquarium. (I must have missed the science class on magnification of heat through glass!)

Spencer insisted on a burial, which I eagerly agreed to, attempting to assuage my guilt at realizing that I had basically fried the poor thing as if it were under a magnifying glass. We put Rex in a suitable container, and went to the backyard. Spencer asked his dad to say a prayer. Trying not to laugh, his dad prayed for Rex to be happy and thanked him for being such a great lizard. After an "Amen," Spencer put his arm around his dad and said, "Now I know how you felt when your grandma died."

Grief is a very interesting emotion. Sorrow and sadness ebb and flow after the death of someone important. What and whom we consider important enough to grieve over is variable. Spencer was devastated by his lizard's death for weeks—we were baffled at his intensity of emotion. He hadn't shown that much emotion in years. We offered a new lizard, but he would have nothing to do with another reptile. I even offered a bigger reptile (which was a significant sacrifice on my part) but he told us he "couldn't even contemplate such a thing."

Coping with grief is an experience all of us will have in our lives. Assuming that an individual with ASD will not experience grief is wrong and dangerous. I was doing a consultation for an adult with ASD recently. Let's call him "Adam." Adam had exhibited rising aggression and outbursts and his staff was uncertain if they could continue to support him within his group home if the aggression didn't stop. I asked when the aggression had begun to escalate, and if anything had occurred at that time. Initially, the staff said that nothing significant had occurred. Later on, while discussing a different topic, one of the staff referenced the time frame of an incident as happening a few months ago "because that was when Keith died." I stopped her and asked about Keith. Keith was a housemate of Adam's. The team then remembered that another housemate passed away a week later. When I asked if Adam had attended the funeral or wake, there were blank looks on their faces. I probed further, asking what discussions had occurred with Adam about death. It became clear that a significant portion of his challenging behaviors and aggression were because of his grief, lack of knowledge about death, and inability to express his grief. I believe that Adam was also confused as to why no one else would talk about Keith anymore. We wrote a social story about death and created supports that allowed him to express his grief. Aggressive behaviors decreased by 87% the next month.

How individuals with ASD cope with their grief can be very different from family and societal expectations. When my father passed away in 2007, we were able to have him at home, surrounded by family at the time of his passing. The boys knew their grandfather was very ill, and would probably die soon. Spencer was teary when his grandfather died and joined us in the family circle surrounding my father. When Joshua entered the room, he had a huge smile on his face. He said, "Is he dead now?" I told him yes, and he responded, "Well, he was very old and nobody lives forever." I know that many people would consider his statement callous and his facial expression highly inappropriate. But we knew Josh and understood that he was trying to make sense of what was happening. Joshua then said, "Don't we need to say a prayer?" After a moment of shock, the rest of our family circle agreed. When the prayer was done, Josh said, "Okay, well, I'm out of here," and he left the room.

My father's funeral was also an interesting insight into the grieving process of a person with autism. We had a private family viewing prior to the funeral service. Spencer was quite tearful and left the room quickly. As he walked outside the viewing room, he saw some family members walking toward the viewing. He asked them if they were going inside and when they responded affirmatively, he said, "Just so you know, there's a dead body in there."

Joshua surprised all of us by approaching his grandfather and saying, "I'm really sorry you are dead, Grandpa, and that I wasn't there for you. I was very worried and anxious and didn't come downstairs to visit much. So I'm very sorry, but I did love you, and you knew that anyway. So that's all I have to say."

I have had families of individuals with ASD share their challenge in helping their child cope with death and grief. One young man took all the pictures of his grandmother off the walls and refused to let her picture be anywhere in the house. He couldn't understand why his mom wanted a picture up of a person who was no longer around. He thought the rule was that you had pictures of people who were alive—because that's the way it had been up to the time of his grandmother's death. Another family was frustrated because after the death of both his parents, a young man wouldn't allow anyone to say their names.

I will never forget the wonderful mother in New York who shared her tragedy of losing her husband in the 9/11 attacks on the World Trade Center. Her young daughter with ASD was in a supported living arrangement at the time, and she had to tell her daughter of her father's death. Because of the media attention surrounding the attacks and the subsequent attention on the funerals, this mother felt that she should not have her daughter attend the funeral, but instead had a small, very private memorial later. Nearly a year afterward, the staff of the residential home asked for a meeting to discuss some challenging behaviors that had increased. The staff was upset at the constant destruction of videotapes and the daughter's obsessive need to stack them. As she was sharing this story with me, this mother began to cry. She related how her daughter was always taking the videotapes and stacking them up into two towers. The "challenging behavior" was part of the grieving and coping process her non-verbal daughter was going through.

At times, an individual with ASD may appear to not have any reactions at all. But humans grieve. And like all of us, people with autism will grieve in their own individual way, and in their own time. We need to be aware of their unusual grief cycle and teach them how to cope with a loss.

Although my boys have not spoken of their grandfather since his passing, each has found a way to keep the memory of their grandfather with him. Spencer wears his grandfather's leather jacket, Josh says he can't sit in the brown recliner because "that was Grandpa's chair," and Zach, I'm certain, talks to Grandpa in his sleep!

STRATEGIES FOR DEALING WITH DEATH AND LOSS

1. Use Clear, Concrete Words to Describe What Has Happened.

While we may want to impart our beliefs about souls and a life hereafter, this information may be too nebulous for a person with ASD. Use statements such as, "Their body couldn't stay healthy" or "their body wouldn't work anymore." The person might need to know that they "won't see Grandma again." If a death has been accidental and unexpected, the person might need to know that their loved one didn't choose to die, and sometimes accidents happen. This concept can be fraught with problems, however, because we use the word "accident" to describe spilled milk also. And spilling milk won't cause death.

2. Accept That Grief Is Different for Everyone.

Changes in behavior, extreme emotions, and verbal statements that don't make sense may all be indicators that the person with autism is experiencing grief.

3. Teach the Social Skills of Death.

The social story format created by Carol Gray is a great way to teach the concepts of death and grief. The person with ASD may need to understand that other people will cry or that they can talk about the dead person. They may need to have the funeral process explained in detail, and told what to do when at the burial itself. Some individuals may need to have a schedule for the funeral if they are attending. Indicate the who, what, where, when, and why of the service, highlighting how the person can tell you if he or she is anxious or fearful.

4. Involve the Person in the Burial.

Depending upon the process chosen for burial, I would strongly recommend that the individual with ASD participate in the funeral in some way. For some individuals, seeing the body of their loved one or friend during a wake is a concrete way to understand that the person will no longer be talking to them or be a part of their life. For others, seeing the casket buried may be an integral part of their coping.

Some individuals may be traumatized by the burial process, and should participate in another way. Small, private memorial services may be more appropriate or visiting the gravesite a month or so later may be a more calming experience. If a person with autism attends the funeral, especially if it is a very young person, consider asking a very close friend to be the child's buddy. During the funeral for my father, I asked a close friend to keep an eye on Josh. If he was getting agitated or needed to take a break during the service, she quietly walked out with him and ensured that his needs were met. This allowed me to participate in the funeral service without worrying about how he was handling it. My husband and I chose not to have Zachary attend the funeral, because we felt he would struggle with my divided attention, and his relationship with his grandfather was not that close. We will make a different decision when his grandmother passes away, because she has been an integral part of his life.

5. Allow for Processing Time.

Grief is a cyclical process that can occur throughout a person's life. A person with autism may exhibit signs of grief days, months, or even years later. Being aware of this will allow for greater understanding of the emotional needs and, hopefully, provide appropriate supports.

PART II

Education

CHAPTER 11

Pyramid Theories:
Choosing Interventions

The five o'clock news reported that six children with autism had been "cured" by taking the vitamin L-Carnitine. By six o'clock, I had fielded seven calls from parents and three calls from education professionals wanting to know if the report was true, and how to get the vitamin. By seven o'clock, I had responded to another 12 calls. According to the autism grapevine, the vitamin would now remove the autism diagnosis from your child's life, have to be bought on the "black market" because of the demand, reduce self-stimulatory behavior, increase language, *and* help bring peace to the Middle East! The next day I was hounded by constant phone calls from around the country wanting to know if the report was correct and if I had bought any of the vitamin. And then there were the phone calls and emails from people asking me why I had never given L-Carnitine to my children—"didn't I want them cured?"

My multiple roles as parent, autism consultant, and educator sent me to the health food store the next day to see what I could find out about the vitamin. As I was browsing the aisle, trying to find anything with the label "L-Carnitine," the manager of the store approached me. She asked if she could help, and then directed me to where I could find the one bottle of L-Carnitine in the store. As the discussion of my interest in the vitamin continued, and I told her of my children, she recommended over 13 vitamins that would "cure" my children. She vehemently insisted that if I did not give my children these vitamins, they were doomed to a life of "silence and misery." She then asked if I had ever done Pyramid Therapy. I had never heard of this intervention, so my puzzled look encouraged her to describe in detail the intervention. According to her, I would need to put my children in a pyramid-shaped tent for three hours, three times per day for three weeks. The pyramid shape would draw the negative energy out of their systems and they would be cured. I thanked her for the information and quickly left the store.

The prevalence of autism in our world means a prevalence of theories and interventions. We hear of interventions in a variety of ways—on a news report, a movie screen, from our second cousin twice-removed, from our doctor, or from the woman-sitting-next-to-you-on-an-airplane. In my relatively small community, I am frequently stopped by people who want to discuss different interventions for autism. Everyone wants to know which intervention will make a difference in the lives of their children. Everyone wants to know what we've tried with our boys. And *everyone* has an opinion on the validity and veracity of each intervention!

We have tried a wide range of interventions with our boys over the past 16 years. Applied Behavioral Analysis, The Lovaas Method, Relationship Development Intervention, Hippotherapy, Speech Therapy, Auditory Integration Therapy, a Gluten-free/Casein-free diet, Enzyme therapy, and Floortime, to name a few. The discussion of each intervention and the connecting thoughts and outcomes is lengthy and best left for a different format. However, I will share what I have learned about the process of choosing an intervention.

First, every child is unique and different—even in the same family and gene pool. Autism intervention is part science and part art. Look at the connection between the science of the intervention and the child's strengths and challenges. Then make the best decision that you can based on the information you have. All of us need to remember that it was only 25 years ago that society believed that autism was caused by the horrible parenting skills of mothers. Bruno Bettelheim's theory of the "Refrigerator Mother" was accepted by society and touted on the major news programs—he would have been a guest on Oprah if he were in today's media world! That doesn't mean he was correct in his theory. And we may find ourselves looking back on our beliefs about autism 25 years from now with the same horror we feel when we think about Bettelheim.

Current research has indicated that the exact type of intervention may not be as critical as the method and format of the intervention. This has been true with our family. We believe that the "success" of my boys has been a combination of many interventions—not just one. The intensity of the intervention, consistency of teaching across locations, planned and thoughtful goals, and a focus on core autism characteristics has provided the most significant and long-term improvements in language, social interaction, and behavior. When choosing an intervention, those involved need to spend a significant amount of time contemplating how the intervention is presented and structured—not just on projected outcome.

Because individuals with autism change and grow, interventions also need to change and grow. As a young child, Joshua responded to Applied Behavioral Analysis instruction immediately with significant increases in language and interaction. However, we did not continue to use ABA for the rest of his life just because it worked when he was young. Intervention methods should be re-evaluated frequently for appropriateness to the person's current needs.

I am hesitant to use the word "success" when talking about interventions because the word has become synonymous with "cure." "Success" does not mean "absence of all signs of autism." Our intended outcome was never for a "cure." We wanted the interventions that we attempted to increase the independence and joy our boys had in their lives. And if the symptoms of their autism decreased in that process, we considered it successful.

The most important and successful intervention method we used? Love. Patience. Respect. Trust. I know it sounds corny. But I believe that our overwhelming love for our amazing guys achieved greater results than any other intervention we tried. I cannot prove it with data collection or standardized tests or charts with graphs. I cannot prove their success with grade point averages, scholarships, or financial review. But I see it in their interactions, hear it in their laughter, and feel it with their hugs.

STRATEGIES FOR CHOOSING INTERVENTIONS

It's important to choose interventions that correlate to your child's strengths and challenges and match your family philosophy and lifestyle. Every family is unique, just as every child is unique. We chose interventions that would help our children move closer to their future goals and matched our family priorities. Our goal was to be open to new ideas, but ultimately to ensure that any intervention would do no harm. Not every intervention delivered the hoped-for outcome; sometimes we didn't choose well. Below are the interventions that we felt had a positive impact on our boys:

1. Applied Behavioral Analysis and The Lovaas Method

When our boys were diagnosed, the only intervention that had shown any replicable success was the Lovaas method. (See resources.) The program we created with the help of the Lovaas trainers would now be considered an Applied Behavioral Analysis program: ABA. With the help of a local disability agency, we created a structured teaching program for the boys. At the start, only Spencer and Joshua were involved because Zachary had not yet spiraled into his autism.

The first week of therapy was hellish, horrible, horrific—you get the idea. But on the tenth day, it clicked for Josh. He calmly walked with his therapist into the teaching room, sat down, and began to show us how truly intelligent he was. Spencer was a bit more compliant, but not by much! We followed a rigid ABA program for about one and a half years.

When Zachary was diagnosed, we started him with ABA. He also received very structured, directed teaching in his educational setting. Zachary did not respond as well to the structure, so we shifted to a different intervention for him after approximately a year, because we were not seeing the progress we wanted.

For all three boys, we saw a significant increase in focus, verbal language, social interactions, and play skills when knowledge and tasks were presented in a visual, structured, concise manner.

2. Speech Therapy

We had speech therapy for all the boys through their Individualized Educational Plans, and private Speech Therapy. Once Spencer and Joshua began using sentences, we continued speech therapy but with a more pragmatic focus. Zachary continued to be non-verbal with delayed echolalia, and speech therapy continued in order to support his learning with an augmentative communication device.

3. Floortime

We incorporated the Floortime* method into the structured teaching times of our home program. This intervention was very positive for Zachary, who had not responded well to the strict ABA setting. All three boys demonstrated an increase in social language, eye contact, and play skills.

*Floortime builds on individuals' innate interests and emotions and is tailored to their unique strengths and challenges. Interactions often start with both the young child and facilitator/parent "playing together" on the floor. The facilitator follows the lead of the child in play, while simultaneously presenting enjoyable, appropriate challenges to increase emotional, social, and intellectual capacities. The program is often used in conjunction with other therapies, as needed, and many parents have testified to its efficacy.

4. Auditory Integration Therapy

We chose the Tomatis method of auditory integration therapy for improving auditory processing and social engagement with all three boys. The process was exhausting—two three-hour sessions a day for 12 days, then a 12-day break, then another set of 12 days. Zachary absolutely hated wearing headphones, so the first few days were particularly challenging for him. Spencer and Joshua weren't happy about keeping the headphones on, but they eventually complied.

Joshua showed the most significant change after the first 12 days. He was quite sensitive to sound prior to the therapy and refused to have music playing in the car, house, or anywhere else. After the first 12-day session, he asked me to turn the radio on in the car, and was humming along. He also spontaneously asked, "How was your day, Dad?" when Craig came home from work. His social interactions increased tremendously.

Spencer showed an increased tolerance for other sensory input, such as allowing his hair to be combed, trying a few new foods, and wearing pants with snaps and buttons. Zachary demonstrated an increase in cheerful attitude—he was just happier in general, not as anxious, with less screaming, and fewer crying spells.

5. Hippotherapy

I love the word that describes horseback riding therapy: *hippotherapy!* The visual picture it creates for me of my boys riding huge, slow, plodding hippos brings such a smile to my face! And then there's the picture of them riding the hippos in water—priceless!

We had Zachary start riding horses through a local hippotherapy group. Our choice was focused on a leisure activity that he could enjoy, not necessarily based on an outcome related to autism. But he really loved riding a horse and we found him willing to put on a helmet, wait his turn, and follow simple directions when those commands were connected to his horse. He said his first after-autism word while on horseback: "Go!"

He wanted his horse to move and we wouldn't tell the horse to move until he tried to say the word.

6. Education

For our family, the most significant intervention in terms of outcome was education. The time, energy, and thought put into their daily program at school had the most long-term success of anything else we have tried. We saw the greatest changes in their autism when we made the commitment to understand the educational system, establish positive relationships with the school team, and focus our energy on ensuring programming that matched their needs and learning styles.

There have been a variety of other interventions that we have dabbled in over the years, but the prior therapies have had the longest longitudinal impact. We have done dietary interventions, enzyme supports, music therapy, art therapy, and tried nearly every gadget, piece of equipment or curriculum we could find and afford. There are some interventions we refused to attempt based upon lack of research and the potential for harm.

CHAPTER 12

The Spectator Sport:
Parent Involvement in Education

I have three athletic brothers and a sports-addicted father. This means that I learned about football, baseball, tennis, and wrestling by spending a lot of my formative years as a spectator. I read *Sports Illustrated* when I was young, and loved it. Baseball was the sport of choice in my home and we had season tickets to the Los Angeles Dodger games.

I eventually became more than a spectator. I learned to "keep the books" for a baseball team—logging hits, runs, strikeouts, and errors. I learned to calculate batting averages and to discriminate between a knuckleball and a slider pitch. Later, I kept the books for my high school varsity baseball team, traveling with them to all of their games. This also means that I learned how to throw a handful of sunflower seeds into my mouth and spit out the shells. Over the years, I have also learned that there are lessons to be gleaned from the game of baseball that transcend the sport—and further, that many of them apply to school life.

The beginning of every school year is difficult and anxiety-ridden for many of us. While it is true that most moms cheer when their kids go off to school, happy for the temporary reprieve as "cruise directors" in charge of entertainment, that same feeling of glee does not always filter down to parents of children with special needs. I'm somewhat happy when my boys go back to school, but I'm also nervous about what the school year will bring.

One year, two of my boys were transitioning into new schools, and so we were all a tad nervous. I fretted and stewed over goals, programming, services, and social rules. I worried about what they would eat for lunch and if their new teachers had enough training to handle their autism. And I worried about whether the new "home team" was actually ready to "play ball."

Over the years, school has become a spectator sport. In the early childhood years, I helped to manage the team, plan strategy, and sometimes, pinch-hit. My input was valued and often required to win the game. In elementary school I was relieved of my managerial duties, but asked to coach first base. My ideas and concerns were discussed at practice sessions (monthly meetings), but for the most part, the game was played daily except for the occasional "steal home" sign from the baseline.

When the boys hit middle school, I felt that I had been sent to the bleachers. At this level it's the teachers and administrators who run the game. For my part (what part?), I was supposed to sit and watch, cheering when my son hit a home run. But most of all, I was expected to applaud a winning season.

Even though I know a lot about this autism "game," and how my sons play on an autism "field," the school personnel didn't want me to coach. Sometimes it felt as if they were saying, "You only coached in the minor leagues. This is the big leagues and we know what we're doing." I wasn't supposed to yell at the umpires (administrators) even when they made a bad call or completely missed the out at 3rd base. School personnel were happy to have me cheer, but questioning the coach or the umpire was unacceptable.

For my part—and yes, I really do want to play a part—I'd like to revert to my position as first base coach, since I know when to tell my boys to steal second, hold a base, or skip third and slide home! I know all the rules of the school "game" too. The "rules" of IDEA (Individuals with Disability Education Act), the state Board of Education, and the local school board are as technical as the rules that define baseball. Other "teams" and "owners" around the country have asked me to "umpire" on a frequent basis. As an umpire (consultant), I can call the players out or safe—and my decision is final. I'm not a rookie at this. I'm a parent and a professional in the autism game. Yet as a parent, if I am frustrated by a call by one of our umpires (administrators), I can't heckle the ump from the bleachers for fear of being asked to leave the park. Schools are good to you as long as you agree with their game strategy.

So as school began, I got ready to become a spectator and a fervent fan of my guys. I learned to bring a blanket and snacks (supports-in-the-ready) in case we went into extra innings. I spent the "pre-season" writing player reports for the new coaches so that they would know what strengths and challenges my players had. The boys and I visited their new "ballparks" (schools) and I helped them find their new "dugouts" (classrooms). I also spent time scouting out other championship teams to see what strategies they were using and how they motivated their players. And I tried very hard not to heckle the umps!

Here's my "field of dreams": I want to play "baseball" on the school team, rather than watch the game from the bleachers. In this version of the game, the teacher, speech-language pathologist, occupational therapist, administrator, and parent would all be coaches who stand, not on the sidelines, but in the middle of the playing field, instructing and encouraging the players from their own unique perspectives, as needed. And all the players (students) would be allowed to play, even if they run the bases backward, don't want to wear their uniforms, or refuse to use a glove. In my perfect school game, no one would keep score, either, because all that matters is that the players love the game.

Being a spectator in the most critical game of our children's lives is not easy. Our amazing kids with autism were given to us to teach, nurture, and coach throughout a lifelong sport. Sitting on the sidelines shouldn't be an option. It helps to know, however, that I don't sit alone in the bleachers. I know that I am surrounded by some of the greatest legends that have ever played the game—other parents. SO, LET'S HEAR IT FOR THE HOME TEAM!

STRATEGIES FOR DEALING WITH YOUR SPECIAL EDUCATION TEAM

1. Know the Rules of the Game.

The rules and laws surrounding special education can be complex. Having at least a basic working knowledge of the rules and regulations that the teachers and support personnel have to work with will allow you to be a positive participant. Take time to learn your state rules and what paperwork is needed to support your child.

2. Attitude Is Everything.

Maintaining a positive, collaborative attitude will ensure that you don't get thrown out of the game! No one goes into education to make a fortune—teachers and administrators truly care about your child. There may be different philosophies or priorities within the team, but everyone is doing the best they can within their ability. Parents are passionate, protective creatures when it comes to their children, as nature designed them to be. Teachers strive to be dispassionate, objective professionals, as their training requires them to be.

3. Keep Focused on Research-based Priorities.

Education for children with autism spectrum disorders should focus on the following priorities:

- Functional, spontaneous communication
- Social skill instruction throughout the day
- Teaching of play skills/imagination
- Cognitive development learning in context
- Intervention to address behavioral challenges
- Academic learning

4. Write Questions Down and Bring Them with You to the Meeting.

This is true for all members of the educational team. In the course of a long meeting, it is easy to forget the questions that you wanted to ask. If you write everything down, you can refer to your questions before leaving the meeting and ensure that your concerns are discussed.

5. Bribery Works!

Bring treats to every meeting. Don't think of it as a bribe—think of it as a reward for the wonderful people who support your child.

CHAPTER 13

Ten Keys for Supporting a Student with Autism

I am frequently asked to give presentations to organizations throughout the U.S. and Canada on educating and raising children with autism. Because the audience members have varying backgrounds and varied knowledge of autism, I needed to synthesize everything I've learned in 18 years into an hour and a half. The following ten "keys" are part of that presentation.

1. Assume Competence.

We took the boys on vacation to Disney World, Florida, in 2003. Now, I know you're surprised, but yes—we go on vacations. And our best friends and their three sons went with us. Yes—we have friends too! And they go on vacation with us! Of course, that's probably because we get that really great disability pass at Disney World that allows you to go right to the front of the line!

On one of our vacation days, we went to Typhoon Lagoon, the water amusement park. My boys were safe in the water, which meant that I could leave them for periods of time without worrying that someone would drown. Zachary didn't swim, but he knew to hold his breath when he went under the water. My girlfriend and I decided to relax on lounges and let our husbands shepherd the boys through water rides and exhibits. One of our friends' sons found us after a while, and asked us to come see the Shark Exhibit with him. As we walked to the exhibit, I asked him where my boys were. He said they were at the Shark Exhibit with the rest of the group.

When I arrived at the Shark Exhibit, I couldn't see my boys. I asked again where my boys were, and my young friend answered, "They're in there." I followed his pointed finger, and realized that all three of my sons were swimming. In water. With snorkeling equipment on. With SHARKS! My first thought was, "Where is their father?" Then, being the quirky parent that I am, I grabbed the camera and took a picture.

As the boys got out of the water, I said to Spencer, "That was awesome! Why did you do that?" He responded, "Everyone else was doing it." I then said to Josh, "But how did you figure out how to do the fins and snorkel?" Josh said, "We just watched what all the other kids were doing." I said, "Well, that was so cool that you went swimming with the sharks!" And Josh yelled, "There were sharks in the water?"

If I had been at the Shark Exhibit when the boys had decided to follow all the other kids and get in the water, I would not have let them do it. I would have found a way to distract them because I didn't think Zach could swim, let alone put on fins and a snorkel! Even I, their greatest supporter, would have assumed that they were incapable of having this great experience.

We used to believe that 80% of individuals with autism were also mentally retarded. We now believe it to be less than 20%. We need to assume that they CAN before we start worrying that they CAN'T.

I frequently listen to educational teams discuss students with autism only in terms of deficit. This not only does the person a disservice, but focusing on deficits does not lead to educational progress. Every person with autism whom I have worked with has been able to do the required task if we find the right way to present the information. We must begin our interactions by assuming competence.

2. Prepare Ahead.

If possible, do an environmental analysis prior to an event. Think about what the person with autism will need to know, do, and say BEFORE you arrive. Teach flexibility within the context of using schedules and lists.

In our home, we used a visual card for Change. It was a bright orange triangle with the word "Change" on it. When a routine became familiar, I would sabotage it, and rearrange the routine on a visual schedule along with the change card placed next to the change on the schedule. For example, if the routine for bed was to 1) go to the bathroom 2) brush your teeth 3) put on pajamas 4) read a book 5) turn lights off, then we would use this visual schedule until the boys were consistent in independently following the schedule. Then I would rearrange the schedule so that visually it was 1) go to the bathroom 2) put on pajamas 3) brush your teeth 4) read a book 5) turn lights off. And I would place the change card next to #2.

The first time you change the routine, it will not go well. Most individuals with ASD don't like change. But it is a necessary skill. Eventually, the person learns that "change" happens sometimes, and it is okay.

Most individuals with autism have a "turnaround time." This is the period of time that it takes them to emotionally handle a change. For some people, handling change can take three minutes. For others, it can take three days. Knowing the student's or child's turnaround time can help you prepare yourself and the person for change.

3. Use a Schedule

This single support is the most successful intervention I have ever used. If a task, event, social situation or behavior is causing difficulty, use a visual. My mantra is: "If at first you don't succeed, make it more visual."

Visual schedules can change behavior. Using visuals will improve attention, decrease anxiety, and increase communication. The consistent use of schedules will provide the person with autism a way to translate and interpret the world around them.

Read the following sentence out loud:

> *"But he's done so well with the schedule,*
> *he doesn't need it anymore."*

That's the last time that I want to hear you say that! Schedules work because they provide the necessary information that the person with autism needs in order to maintain emotional stability.

When I am doing a consultation, I always ask to see the visual supports being used with the person or student. And I frequently have the above sentence said to me. Can you see the humor in this? There was an intervention that worked, but it was removed, and now there are problems again. Hmmm.

Using a schedule is a lifelong skill. Every successful person uses some kind of a schedule—a calendar, a notebook, a Blackberry, an iPad, a written list. Imagine what would happen if I told you that, because you completed your activities the day before, I was going to take your calendar away. The only change to be made to an ASD student's schedule is to make it more age-appropriate. But NEVER take it away!

4. Teaching Options Is Critical.

Generalizing information is difficult for many people with autism. We had taught Zachary to swim in our local pool, and he was doing great. But when we went on a vacation to the Atlantic Ocean, he had no idea what to do. We needed to teach him all over again how to swim in water, because it wasn't the SAME water.

Individuals with autism need their teachers to be more flexible and more creative than they are! Demonstrating knowledge doesn't always need to be done in a report, or on a test. Focus on what specific knowledge the student is supposed to know, and then think of how he or she can share that knowledge with you. Most students with ASD have significant test anxiety, and will not show their actual knowledge in that format.

Matching the curriculum to the student's special interest is vital to providing motivation in difficult subjects. When Josh was in the 4th grade, the history curriculum used in his class went through American history by region. The students learned about the history of the East, then the South, then the Midwest, etc., from the first settlers until the present day. This was particularly difficult for Josh, because there wasn't a sense of continuity. We decided to use his fascination with trains, and had him write or draw the progression of trains and the railroads through the settling of America. He was ecstatic, and learned American history at the same time. His drawings served as the visual cues to describe what he had learned to his classmates.

5. Know Your Support Team.

Individuals with autism will have challenging behaviors. It's part of the diagnosis. It is vital to know the people who can help when the person is struggling. The titles of the support team may include teacher, speech pathologist, social worker, counselor, physician, parent, behaviorist, principal, or custodian. What they do on a daily basis isn't as important as what their relationship is with your child or student. Know their names, their phone numbers, their birthdays, and what kind of cookies they like. Establishing a positive relationship with these individuals will ensure that when life begins to overwhelm the person with autism (and you!) there are people ready to help.

For family members, it is also critical to establish your personal support team. Find a support group, blog, chat room, or some other avenue to connect with other families who live with autism. Everyone needs a friend who understands them. Find the people who provide the emotional support that you need. Create positive relationships with all the professionals involved in your life. They can help access resources, connect you to other families, and become your next best friend!

6. Have Typical Peers Available for Friendship.

One of the greatest myths about people with autism is that they don't care about other people or want to connect with others. This is not true! Individuals with autism want to have friends—they just don't know how to do it.

Teaching social interaction skills is critical to lifelong success and happiness. Our children and students will be able to "do" a job, but they won't be able to *get* the job or *keep* the job if they don't know how to behave appropriately in the break room or with customers.

Having consistent, positive interactions with typically developing peers provides the environment needed to generalize skills taught in therapy or the classroom. Supporting these interactions by teaching scripts, social rules, expected and unexpected behaviors, will improve the likelihood of finding a friend.

Friendship, for all of us, is based upon shared interests. This can be fairly difficult for a person with autism who may be interested in electrical towers or North American mammoths. But wherever possible, find other individuals who enjoy spending time discussing the person's passion.

There are age rules to friendship, however. A sophomore in high school cannot be friends with a kindergartner, even if they both love dinosaurs. The social-age rule of friendship changes slightly when an adult, but a person who is 30 still cannot spend too much time with a six-year-old. Teaching these age rules, clearly and concisely, will ensure that the friendship is appropriate. The rule that I use is that a friend can be your age, or one year older, or one year younger.

In a classroom setting, it is helpful to create positive environments for friendship. The scariest words to a student with autism are "Everyone choose a partner." At this statement, the person with autism may begin going through their mental "file cabinet" of fellow students, thinking of their names, their faces, and whether they will complete the assignment appropriately or not. By the time the student with autism is finished thinking of all these issues, everyone else has chosen a partner and he or she is left working alone. Or working with the adult in the room. Assign groups, and structure the assignment clearly, so there is no opportunity for argument.

Sometimes, the priority for a classroom or group activity should be having the student engage with others socially—not actually do the assignment. Spencer's teacher once told me that when given a choice of working in a group or working alone, he will always choose to work alone. When I asked Spencer about this, he said, "I can't do the work and talk at the same time. And you want me to get an A, Mom, so I choose to do the work." Asking the student to focus on the social interaction, instead of completing the work, is just as hard as it is for other students to complete the assignment.

In the research done on bullying, the one characteristic most likely to make a student the target for bullies is *not* talking differently, dressing differently, or making unusual noises. It's being *alone*. Having one friend is critical. Having two friends is great. More than that? A bonus. That's why teaching social interaction skills is so critical to the education and life of students with ASD.

7. Be Aware of Sensory Needs.

Sensory processing challenges are found in almost all individuals with autism. Most individuals have difficulty processing lights, sounds, smells, certain touches, or tastes. The majority of individuals I work with are hypersensitive to sensory input. Some are hyposensitive: they don't have any reaction to the sensory input.

Our son Zachary is hypo-sensitive to temperature. We would find him outside in only a pair of shorts when it was -20°. He would put on a winter coat, hat, gloves, and boots in the middle of summer if told to. There are significant safety issues with being hypo-sensitive to the senses. This challenge can be exhibited by individuals who eat constantly (no response to feeling full), no response to having a bowel movement in their diaper (no response to smell), or it might be a limited response to a fall, or a cut in their skin (no response to touch.) But most individuals with autism are hypersensitive to sensory input and have strong reactions to common smells, sounds, fabrics, or foods.

Autism spectrum disorder is a neurological disorder; the brain's neurons are firing differently than a typically developing person's. This frequently results in a limited ability to process all the senses at one time. Most of us can tolerate a classroom, for example, that has bright fluorescent lights, sunlight, and maybe an overhead projector going at the same time. The classroom will also have a multitude of sounds such as chairs scraping, pencils scratching, other students in the hallways, and whispering in the back of the classroom. While in the class, we tolerate the feel of a chair underneath us, and clothing that may or may not be keeping us warm on any given day. Simultaneously, we can probably smell the person next to us (let's hope it's a good smell!), and the cafeteria lunch being prepared. And in the midst of all this information coming into our brain, simultaneously, we know that the most important thing to focus on is . . . the teacher. Amazing. Our brain takes the sights, sounds, smells, and touches, and files the information in some part of our brain called "things-I-don't-need-to-think-about-right-now." The person with autism may not be able to do this. Their brain may be telling them to focus on the fact that the overhead projector is making a very different noise or the fact that there is a tag still in their shirt and it's bothering them.

When this challenge of processing sensory input is taken into consideration, the struggle to cope with changing environments makes more sense (pun intended!). And the shifting of seasons, clothing, and temperature can cause significant behavioral challenges.

Providing frequent opportunities to re-organize themselves, visuals to predict changing weather and environment, and sensory integration activities will assist the person with autism in processing sensory input.

8. Schedule Time Alone to Relax.

I wish I had a dime for every time a parent tells me that their child's school team says they don't have any problems at school, but the parent says that when the child arrives home they are "bouncing off the walls." The school day is incredibly difficult for a student with autism. The hours at a job are sometimes almost more than the person with autism can handle. They are expending more energy and brainpower than neuro-typical individuals in order to complete the task, finish a job, and speak with the others around them. When they arrive home, all the stress and tension of the day bursts out, and the result may be seen in the behavioral challenges upon arrival at home.

A person with autism needs the opportunity to spend time alone.

We frequently forget how vital this is to their emotional stability. In our home, we found that when the boys got home from school, they needed to be left alone—not made to sit down and do homework. Our schedule gave the boys a minimum of 45 minutes to engage in their favorite technology. After they had time to be alone, and relax, then they were able to complete homework, engage with us at mealtime, and do their evening activities. And we nearly eliminated the "after-school meltdown."

Some individuals with autism may find themselves at the point of "meltdown" during the course of the school or workday. Those children who bolt and run from the room are frequently at the end of their ability to cope with the stress of interactions. Two of our boys were "runners" for a period of time. Zachary, in particular, was quick and likely to bolt and run at the instant that he started to be overwhelmed. We found that if we chose the place that we wanted him to run to, we could at least ensure that he was safe when he ran.

Working with Zach's educational team, we chose a location at school that was acceptable and safe. And then we taught Zach to run to that location. We showed him a visual card of the place we wanted him to go, and then held his hand and ran with him to the chosen spot. The chosen spot had things that calmed him—not favorite toys or books—but calming items. We practiced running to his chosen spot frequently. And he quickly began to run there when he was very upset—not out the door, or into the street, or into another classroom.

9. Have a Communication System Available at All Times.

In times of stress, the ability to speak decreases. This is a physiological response to increased adrenalin. When adrenalin increases, the chemical needed in the language part of the brain decreases. Have you ever been having an argument with someone, and when it was over, you thought to yourself, "I should have said____"? We struggle with our verbal language when we are frustrated, or angry, or scared.

People with autism are stressed for most of their day. So their ability to use their verbal language, which is delayed or impaired to begin with, is decreased.

A communication system needs to be available at all times, and should support the ASD person's worst day. This means that if the person with autism typically uses verbal language to communicate, they might need written scripts on a very difficult day. If the person uses written communication, they may need picture communication on a really difficult day. The communication system in place needs to be easy, immediately available, and efficient when emotions are out of control.

There should also be a communication system available for all those involved with the person with autism to communicate with each other. Parents should ask their child's educational team what communication system is best for the team—email, phone calls, written notes, etc. Individuals at work sites should ask their supervisor what form of communication is most effective to discuss concerns. Making plans for a communication system—ahead of a crisis—will ensure a speedier resolution to a difficult moment.

10. Have Fun!

People with autism are amazing, wonderful, frustrating, fabulous individuals. They want to enjoy their life. They want to be with people who enjoy them. Working with, and living with, people with autism will be the greatest experience you will ever have. Embrace the opportunity and enjoy the experience!

Most of my consultation focuses on changing behavior. All behavior is communication. Using these "keys" will reduce and eliminate the challenging behaviors because they support the learning and understanding that the person with autism needs.

CHAPTER 14

Scheduled Grief: Individualized Education Plans

I 'm unsure of the exact count, but I believe I have attended over 125 Individual Education Plan meetings in the past 17 years. And those are just the IEP meetings for my own children! If I counted the additional meetings I've attended as a consultant, the number would probably reach 300.

This should mean that IEP meetings are routine, unemotional events in my life. True. Most of the time. But I'm the mother of children with autism, so my emotional stability at an IEP is directly correlated to the emotional stability and academic success of my children. Knowing the federal education law inside and out does not prevent my anxiety from rising if I am concerned about the math curriculum. Having a solid, positive relationship with the educational team doesn't guarantee that there won't be hurt egos when I question the validity of the proposed behavioral plan. All my consultant expertise is diminished by my emotions when it comes to my own children.

I call IEP meetings "Scheduled Grief." Every year, at least once, I will be required to sit in a room and listen to a variety of professionals discuss how my children are different than other students. I will spend a minimum of two hours reviewing test scores that appear to indicate that my child is below average, or not capable of completing the statewide tests to begin with. I am guaranteed to go through at least part of the grieving cycle, if not all the phases. And I will have to put it on a calendar.

There have been years when I am at the stage of acceptance in the grief cycle and an IEP meeting is relatively calm. There have been years when I am in the denial phase, and the slightest indication of deficit about my child will launch me into a tirade about the lack of support and interventions provided. And there have been years when I am in the sadness phase of grieving and an IEP meeting requires a whole box of Kleenex.

Because our boys were at the same elementary school for nearly seven years, I spent many IEP meetings with the same educational professionals. We used to jokingly call it "Beytien IEP Day" because we would schedule all three IEP's in the same day. I would sit in the room, while the various team members would rotate in and out of it, changing documents in front of me, and replenishing my Diet Coke. We had a fabulous educational team, and the IEP meetings were mostly collaborative and supportive.

One year, during a relatively uneventful IEP meeting for Josh, my grief overwhelmed me. I can't remember what was specifically said—

whatever was said wasn't connected to my emotional outburst. But somehow, in the middle of a discussion, the tears began. The educational team had never seen me lose control within a meeting. My obvious distress stopped them cold. I had to leave, and pull myself together in the bathroom. When I entered the room again, the silence was absolute. The expressions on the team's faces ranged from horror to worried to uncomfortable. I tried to explain that it wasn't their fault, that I was just overwhelmed by the challenges still ahead of my family.

Federal Law, No Child Left Behind, and numerous other state and local regulations combine to create an antagonistic environment for parents and school professionals alike. What should be a conversation and a discussion of strengths, challenges, and supports has become a rigid format of test scores, behavior problems, and attempts to prove or disprove the need for services. Parents are left as supplicants at the altar of education, begging for their child to be taught and often not knowing what they can even ask for. Teachers' insights and opinions are often sidelined and marginalized for the sake of budgetary concerns.

But the process doesn't have to be this way. Each of us—parents, teachers, administrators, speech pathologists, occupational therapists, paraprofessionals, and any other person involved in the education of a person with autism—can ensure that an IEP meeting stays focused on the needs of the student. Here are some strategies to make this happen both philosophically and practically:

Strategies for Managing the IEP

Philosophy:

1. Be Proactive.

When everyone accepts responsibility for their part of the student's learning, then there is an attitude of collaboration and cooperation. Parents should acknowledge that a school team cannot teach a child everything that child needs to know and learn. Teachers should acknowledge that school encompasses the largest portion of the child's day and is the most important social environment the student will have.

2. Be Forward Thinking.

Start each IEP meeting talking about the student's future. Where does the student and his or her family want to finish when their school days have ended? Then work backward toward a single year's goals.

3. Be Focused.

Schools cannot teach everything. Prioritize goals in order to create a clear, mutual understanding of what needs to be accomplished in the course of a school year. It is more effective to focus the team's energy toward measurable results on three goals than it is to have limited results on eight goals. Focus on what goals need to be accomplished first, then discuss how to accomplish those goals.

4. Be Collaborative.

Work toward consensus whenever possible. Consensus is not compromise. Each team member may have different philosophies of what is important for the child. The most successful school teams accept the different philosophies and work toward consensus and understanding. The old adage "Think before you speak" is critical in IEP meetings with differing opinions.

5. Be Understanding and Understood.

Listen with the intent to understand, not with the intent to respond. Parents should remember that no one chooses education as a career because they will make a ton of money. Teachers should remember that no parent chooses to have a child with autism. Everyone at the meeting believes he or she has the child's best interests in mind. The goal isn't necessarily to agree, but to understand the other's viewpoint.

6. Be Unified.

Once a set of goals and focus is agreed upon, every member of the team should be supportive and give their best effort toward accomplishing the goals. Constant negativity, suspicion, and unsupportive remarks will undermine the success of the student and the success of the team.

7. Be Positive.

Everyone needs to know that they are valued and important. Give compliments, write notes of thanks, highlight success, and give credit when it is due. And that goes for parents *and* educators. Rewards are part of *everyone's* behavior plan!

Practicality for Teachers

1. Individual Education Plans are lengthy, complicated documents. Schedule more than 30 minutes for an IEP meeting. Ninety minutes is the average time needed for an annual education meeting to support a student with autism.

2. Provide draft copies at least three days prior to the meeting. Everyone needs to have an opportunity to read and review all documentation prior to the meeting. This allows for questions to be formed, other documentation to be brought to the meeting, and will keep the meeting on schedule.

3. Arrange the seating at the meeting so that the parents are seated next to the person with the documentation. This ensures that the parents have the appropriate documentation and are literally on the same page as everyone else. Also, never seat the parents on one side of a table, and the school team on the other side. That arrangement almost always ends up in a Due Process hearing!

4. Understand that parents are passionate, protective creatures when it comes to their children, as nature designed them to be.

Practicality for Parents

1. Write a summary of your child's success and challenges at home and in the community. Also write what has been successful during the past school year and what has been challenging. This information is important to add into the documentation of an IEP so that there is a clear record of generalization of skills outside of the school setting. Parents can add this "report" into the IEP document.

2. Write a list of questions and comments prior to the IEP meeting. Writing questions down is critical because emotions can sometimes sidetrack you, and if all of the questions don't get answered before the meeting is done, then another meeting can be scheduled.

3. Always bring another person with you to the meeting. A close friend, spouse, or relative—someone who can help you process what is happening, stay unemotional, and be supportive.

4. Bring treats. Seriously. Even if the treats aren't eaten during the meeting, the team will appreciate them later. I don't call it "bribery"—I call it positive reinforcement!

5. Understand that teachers strive to be dispassionate, objective professionals, as their training requires them to be. They have many students to teach and the current education system overloads them with additional tasks.

6. Learn all that you can about state and federal education law. Knowledge is power and knowledge brings serenity. IEP meetings are less stressful when you understand the process and the parameters.

CHAPTER 15

Moving On Up:
Transitions in Education

I t was the first day of school, 1996. Four-year-old Joshua was heading
off to an early childhood special education class, and Spencer, five,
was heading off to kindergarten. I was headed for a nervous breakdown!

When the school bus pulled up to our home that first morning, my
stress level went from zero to sixty! It was a BIG bus—not the small,
special education bus I had been expecting, but a full-size bus, teeming
with excited students and exploding with noise. It was the worst
possible place for my four-year-old with autism. With trepidation, I put
him on the bus, turned around (so he wouldn't see me), and burst into
tears. I looked at my husband and said, "Get in the car and follow him!"
My husband looked as if he would refuse—it was only four blocks for

heaven's sake—but he reconsidered when he saw the hysterical "do-not-cross-the-mom" look in my eyes.

Joshua was fine that day. And the boys have been fine every year on the first day of school. Yet that never seems to relieve my anxiety. The first day of a school year is one of the most stressful for me. Everything is new for my guys, and for me. Individuals with autism typically do not handle transitions well—and neither do some of their parents! There were times when I drove around town, certain that I would be called back to school because one of the boys couldn't handle the day. Other times I paced in front of the school for hours on the first day, unable to leave in case I forgot to put something in the boys' backpacks. And when my oldest son drove himself and his brother to high school? Oh yeah—I followed them that time too!

I've done everything I can to help ease their transition—and mine—into a new school year. I understand the reality of school life for educators. My mom was a teacher for over 30 years, so I know what goes on behind the scenes. I know that a teacher may have read the IEP, but may not remember every little piece of it. So I always send a brief note with the "Ten Things to Know about (Spencer, Joshua, or Zachary)." This allows me to give the educational team the nitty-gritty things they need to know about my child (e.g., *Don't touch his head;* or *He is currently quoting* 101 Dalmations; or *He doesn't tolerate someone telling him to be quiet*). Every parent knows that these are the types of things that are critical for teachers to know, and they're not in the IEP.

One of the essential pieces of information about Zachary, our youngest son with autism, is that if he holds his hand up to you and says, "Go Away!" you should obey him. Because Zachary has struggled with physical aggression since the onset of his autism, we have taught him to say this when he is feeling edgy. He has learned it well, which is a really good thing. At the start of every school year, I remind his team of this skill, and their need to honor what he says.

A few years ago, we had made the huge transition to a new state, new home, and new school relatively well. The second school year had just begun, and that transition was also going well. My husband and I were out shopping one evening when we spotted a T-shirt with the following message: *What part of GO AWAY don't you understand?* We thought the saying was hilarious, given its connection to Zach, so we bought it for him. Zach wore it to school the next day. As I took him to meet his teacher at the school door, I pointed to his T-shirt and commented that Zach's dad and I have an odd sense of humor. She chuckled and asked, "Did Mrs. Anderson call you last night?"

Mrs. Anderson, whom I had not yet met, was the new principal of the elementary school. Zach's teacher proceeded to tell me that during lunch the previous day Mrs. Anderson approached Zach and asked him if he liked his lunch. He looked at her and said, "Go Away!" She said to him, "No, I'm not going to go away. I want to talk to you about your lunch." So he slugged her! Interesting timing, considering that Zach showed up the very next day, wearing a T-shirt that says, *What part of GO AWAY don't you understand?*

After the incident, Mrs. Anderson immediately walked up to Zach's teacher and said, "What was I thinking?" She was his staunchest supporter and is a fabulous educator and principal.

Transitions between grades and schools are all difficult—difficult for the kids, and difficult for parents. Sometimes I think the IEP should include a transition plan for the parents as well as the student!

My husband and I have weathered a lot of transitions at this point in our lives. As I write this, I am remembering when Spencer, our oldest son (now twenty), was only two days away from graduating from high school. I certainly wasn't "ready" for it—but transitions happen, whether we are ready or not. Do you think I should send a "Ten Things" list to his college professors?

Below is the list I created for Zachary's teachers in 2007. Perhaps it will help you create your own "Ten Things."

Ten Things to Know about Zachary

1. Zachary responds to positive praise.

Zach watches facial expressions and responds to happy encouraging faces. He also works well when encouraged verbally, e.g., "You can do it." "Wow, look at you!" "Great work Zach!" "You did it!"

2. Zachary likes jumping and deep pressure.

Pressing on his hands, rubbing his back, rolling in a barrel, jumping on a trampoline, small doses of weighted vests or tubes, deep shoulder pressure and tickling are all options for sensory integration and calming. Do not give him light touches!

3. Zachary constantly seeks attention.

Zachary will use both positive and negative behaviors to gain attention if he thinks he is not getting what he needs. He will seek out interaction with a preferred person by smiling at them, scripting with them, and standing very close. On the negative side, he will scream or whine or squeeze your wrists if he is not getting across his needs.

4. Zachary does a lot of scripting.

Not all of it understandable! But you might hear phrases from the Shrek, SpongeBob and quite a few other movies. He uses his scripts to verbally respond to situations, so be prepared for some great language to come out at certain moments. Zach likes to have others participate in the script, so let me know if I can help translate!

5. Zachary learns by watching.

Zachary is constantly watching others and what they do. It is how he learns. New tasks should always be demonstrated first, either by a teacher or peer. Any hand-over-hand teaching should be accomplished at his side, not behind him. He will watch how peers do things, and typically follow their lead, especially if it is a motivating task. He will watch the routines of adults and often mimic them perfectly to accomplish the same task. This also means that he is a "policeman" and will physically ensure that other students do what the teacher says!! Watch for this.

6. Zachary protests by whining in a high pitch.

This sound or series of sounds typically precedes a challenging behavior. He is indicating protest and refusal. We prompt with "I want...." By holding a single finger up while saying I, a second finger while saying want, and then hold up a 3rd finger and remain silent. Then wait. If that is not successful, get out the visuals! This whine can escalate into arm squeezing, pinching behind your upper arms, or hitting you on the shoulder.

7. Zachary responds to "yes or no" questions.

For familiar tasks and environments, Zachary is successful with verbal prompts only. However, I would assume that he would need a picture and written cue for the initial months here at school. Whenever possible, break down requests or queries to a "yes or no" question. Example: "Zach, do you want to take a break? Yes or no?" He will respond appropriately.

8. Zachary does not like people to tell him "SHHH" or "No."

Although Zachary can get loud at inappropriate times, telling him "Sshh" and holding a finger to your lips will cause him to hit you. I don't know why, but this is something to warn all other teachers about.

9. Zachary loves to be moving.

His favorite thing is to wander, play, run, or do anything outside. He likes to swim, or take long walks. He should have frequent opportunities to move throughout his day.

10. Zachary is loved by his family.

Absolutely anything we can do to assist in Zach having a

positive experience at school is at the top of our list. He is a cheerful, funny, loving boy who really wants to do what is right and learn. Please contact me with any questions, concerns, ideas, and great stories! We will help in any way we can.

STRATEGIES FOR DEALING WITH EDUCATIONAL TRANSITIONS

1. Write a Social Story.

Use pictures of the school, playground, lunchroom, etc., and write a story telling your child that there will be some new things at school like his teacher, his classmates, and his room, but that some things will be the same, such as the playground, the lunchroom, and the school secretary.

2. Volunteer at School.

Volunteer in the library one day a week; offer to coordinate a field trip; or offer to cut out schedule pictures and laminate them. Volunteering not only shows the school team that you are supportive of their efforts, it also gives you the opportunity to see how the school runs, and to divert potential challenges.

3. Prepare Your Own Top Ten List.

Write a very brief list of your child's current critical issues. Include the things you most want the teacher to know.

4. Set Up a Communication Plan.

Ask the teacher what method of communication he or she prefers—home-school notebook, phone call, or email. Teachers and staff have incredibly busy days, and it may not be possible for them to communicate with you every single day, but at least once a week is essential. Make sure that you are communicating, as well.

5. Positive Praise Works for Everyone.

Families should always take time to highlight when things have gone well, as we surely do when they haven't! Write a letter to the principal if your teacher has made an extra effort. Thank the teacher in person or in a note when you see him or her respond well to a challenging moment.

6. Raise Autism Awareness for Peers.

I am a huge advocate for telling the rest of the class about autism, whether this is done generically or by specifying the child's name (with parental consent, of course). Either way, it is beneficial to have someone discuss the challenges of autism, and help students understand how to respond to those challenges. I have done this every year for my own guys, and I also do a presentation to a large number of classes every year. By being proactive regarding awareness you can help your child gain the patience and support of his or her peers.

CHAPTER 16

Independence Day: Toileting and Self-Care

"Good evening ladies and gentleman, and welcome to the annual Independence Day games! Tonight we are coming to you live from the site of the next Independence Day competition—Toilet Training! Who do we have competing tonight, Bob?"

"Well, Ron, tonight we have Spencer and his mom, Alyson. This ought to be an interesting round of toilet training, Bob. Spencer is four years old, has had chronic constipation, and is highly resistant to any interference by his mom. This mom has her work cut out for her, Bob. So let's head to the bathroom arena and join the competition in progress."

Spencer struggled with constipation his whole life. A diet of waffles, fries, Cheerios and pancakes didn't lend itself to the smooth release he needed. I tried everything—over-the-counter laxatives, enemas, prescription laxatives, herbal remedies, castor oil, and anything else that could possibly help. Bowel movements took hours, and caused constant tears. By the time Spencer was four and a half, I had found an herbal concoction that really helped. So it was time to toilet train.

Spencer loved small action figures so I bought about 20 and put them inside a decorated box. Then I did my "Vanna White" routine, showing him the box of toys and telling him that he could get a toy every time he has a BM in the toilet. Three days later he was independent at toileting!

> "Here we are again Ron, at the next round of the toilet training competition in the Independence Day Games. And back for another match-up is Alyson Beytien!"
>
> "That's right, Bob. She has another child to toilet train, and let me tell you, this one is going to give her a run for her money! Her second son, Joshua, is proving more difficult than Spencer. Let's join the competition in progress."

Joshua would be dry throughout the morning at his Early Childhood class, then come home, scream, yell, and refuse to go near the bathroom, and be wet an hour later. Sigh. I could not find a reward that mattered to him. Then, one day while at the grocery store, he came unglued because I wouldn't buy him a sucker. Ding ding ding! I found the reward!

I put a jar of suckers on top of the toilet tank, secured with Super Glue so it couldn't be moved, and with a metal latched lid that he couldn't open. When Joshua came home from school, I started to walk him into the bathroom, and he started screaming and throwing himself to the floor. I carried him into the bathroom, a flailing mass of hysteria, and showed him the jar of suckers. Stopped him dead in his tracks. He said "Sucker?" I said, "First pee in the potty, then sucker" while showing him the visual pictures. More screaming. More repetition of First/Then. More screaming. Then silence. Joshua sobbed out, "Potty first, then sucker." And went to the bathroom in the toilet.

"Round three of the competition begins tonight, Bob, and there are many who are betting that Alyson cannot repeat her success with the prior two boys."

"It would be a miracle if she does, Ron. Zachary is a difficult child with many more challenges, so the difficulty level has tripled. Alyson's not going to be able to rest on her past successes in this round of the competition. There are many who say she should have waited another year or two before attempting the toileting."

"Well, we'll see whether her determination and sheer stubbornness can win Zach over to independently toileting. It will be a great night at the Independence Day games!"

I was certain that I could toilet train Zach. Every night, after I had put him to bed, he would get up, strip naked, and go back to sleep. And he would get up in the morning, completely dry. After he would get a diaper put on him, he would soak the diaper. So I figured it was an appropriate time to start. My plan was to not put a diaper on him in the morning, but take him to the bathroom and wait him out. I knew that Zach had a 24 hour learning curve. He would spend 24 hours angry and miserable anytime we changed his life in an attempt to teach him something new, and then he was fine.

However, after four days I was certain that I would never be able to toilet train this boy! Not only did my plan fail miserably, it set off constant aggression from Zach towards me. On the fifth day, I told Craig that I couldn't keep going. Craig offered to take a day off from work, and help Zach and me get through the plan.

Zach woke up, dry and naked, and Craig took him into the bathroom. I figured we could push his bladder to capacity and make him happy by giving him some root beer soda. Craig took the two liters of soda in with him, closed the door, and repeatedly showed Zach the visual for toileting. Nothing. Zach screamed and yelled at us. Hours later and still—nothing. Zach has now gone nearly 15 hours without urinating. He looks like a starving child from Ethiopia. He is miserable and so are we.

Craig steps out of the bathroom to take a business call, and I take his place. Zach is furious with me—looking right at me and screaming. I said, "Zach, I love you. You can do this." The tears began to roll down my face. Zach yelled at me, then walked over to the toilet and peed. I was so excited that I yelled out my excitement. He was still peeing, but then turned to me and said, "No yelling!"

Zach never had a toileting accident after that.

"Just when you thought the Independence Day competition couldn't get any more difficult, we bring you the Teenager

Tournament! In this competition, the competitors have to teach their children all the skills needed for living life as a teenager. The competitors can choose a single skill for each teenager, or they can add multiple skills for added difficulty and points."

"And this is where the current reigning champ, Alyson Beytien, will have all her skills put to the test. She's chosen to teach Spencer to drive and shave, Joshua to do the laundry and take out the trash, and Zachary to make his bed and vacuum his room. I'm not sure she can pull this off, Bob."

"Ron, I think you are underestimating her focus and skill at creating visual systems. When I spoke with her the other day before the start of the games, she told me that she was determined that her guys would not live with her for the rest of her life. Independence in these skills will be critical to achieving her goals."

I am a firm believer that every person needs to work. Collaborative work teaches critical social interaction skills, perspective-taking, and the importance of completing what you start. We have had the boys do chores at home since they were at least six years old. We found that teaching a routine for completing a list of chores every Saturday morning helped to instill in them a work ethic. Initially, each boy had a short list of chores to complete, with our direct instruction and supervision. When they were able to complete their list without instruction, we taught them to cross off their chores and bring the list to us to review.

The boys eventually learned to complete a variety of chores, all written on a list on Saturday morning. From yard work, to cleaning out the garage, to cleaning bathrooms, and doing the laundry, we were diligent in teaching them to be independent. Spencer liked to tell people that I had children so that I could have slaves! They were motivated to learn by the reward; once the chores were completed, I would not ask them to do anything else for the rest of the day. They could play video games, watch movies, or play with trains for the remainder of their Saturday. This guaranteed their cooperation.

A few months ago, we were at my in-laws helping to clean out their garage. The boys worked with us and we were finished in less than four hours. My mother-in-law expressed to Spencer her surprise that we were done so quickly. Spencer told her, "Well, we're Beytiens!" She said, "I'm a Beytien too, and I haven't been able to get this garage cleaned for years!" Spencer responded, "But you weren't raised by my mom!"

While I adore my guys, I don't believe that they should live with me for the rest of their lives. My goal is to prepare my sons for dealing with life when I'm no longer here. They deserve the opportunity to choose where and with whom they live. They deserve to make their own mistakes, choose their own friends, and choose their own leisure activities. Teaching them to be independent in all areas of their life will allow them to have those choices and not be limited by what they can't do.

"Well, Bob, another round of competition is over and it looks like Alyson Beytien may actually win this game."

"I wouldn't speak too soon, Ron. This competition for independence lasts for years, and there are some difficult rounds ahead. She'll have to stay focused to actually win this game. And she's got some of the most challenging rounds ahead of her."

"I'll look forward to seeing you at the next round of competition, Bob. And I'll look forward to watching Alyson work through the challenges. Maybe we'll get to see her win the gold medal."

"That's it for now. Tune in for the next round of competition!"

I still have skills to teach my guys, and tasks that I need to hand over to them. Life continually brings new skill needs, and new levels of independence. We'll keep working and "competing" in this arena.

And one day, I will happily accept the gold medal for winning in the Independence Day games!

STRATEGIES FOR TEACHING INDEPENDENCE

1. Use Visuals.

How many times have I said this? Individuals with autism are typically highly visual learners. The strategy of making a task, event, or learning concept visual has always been the first thing I turn to when the person with autism is struggling. Don't just tell them what to do—SHOW them what to do.

The key purpose for using a visual system is independence.

Visual systems promote independence because a picture can always be available even when a support person is not. People with autism will understand a task better with a visual representation and they will be able to complete it without a support person standing next to them.

2. Everyone Needs Work.

Work builds brain tissue. Work builds social skills. Work builds a positive outlook on life. Work builds self-worth. Work is critical to life-long happiness. The type of work is not important; work at home, work at school, or work at a place of employment will all provide the needed input for improvement.

Young children are capable of clearing their plates off the table, putting away clean dishes, emptying trash cans, or picking up toys. Many young children with autism love to work outside helping to pull weeds, plant flowers, rake leaves etc. Yard work is a terrific "heavy work" activity to assist in sensory processing.

3. Step away from the Child!

Children with autism *can be independent*. Sometimes, we are unaware of how much we are helping people with autism and failing to see that we need to allow them to do more for themselves. Sometimes, parents get into dependence routines without knowing it: dressing the ten-year-old for school, always making breakfast for the 20-year-old, or putting the child's shoes and coat away every day. Review your child's daily routine and decide which activities they can accomplish alone—if you teach them.

4. Independent Skills are Free.

Any task or activity that requires a "staff" person to assist will cost, at minimum, an additional $5,000 per year. For example, if your child needs help with doing his or her laundry and it takes one hour each week to do the laundry at a rate of $10 per hour, then that support person will cost a minimum of $5,200 per year. Now add in the other tasks that your child needs help with and add up the additional cost per year. Teaching independent skills will save money, and ensure that the money the person does have is used for living the life they want—not paying other people.

5. Independent Skills Today Yield More Options Tomorrow.

The more independent people with autism are with their daily living and work skills, the more choices they will have regarding where they live and how they spend their days. The goal for families and professionals should be to lose their jobs! If our children and students are independent, and we aren't needed anymore, we have done our jobs.

The most critical independent skill is toileting and bathing. Some individuals may need months or years of teaching to accomplish these skills independently, but it will be time well spent. Being independent in toileting and self-care will ensure that a variety of options are available to the person later in life, and it will give them added protection against abuse. If the student or child is not currently toilet-trained, make it a priority goal. Everything else can wait.

CHAPTER 17

So You Want to Be an Expert: Studying Autism

I vividly remember telling my mom that I wanted to be an *expert* in something. I didn't really know what I wanted to be an expert in at the time. I was a senior in high school and contemplating my future and career. My mom asked me what I thought I wanted to focus on in college, and I told her that I was tired of being good at a lot of things, but not an expert in anything. (If you listen closely, you will hear the "heavens" laughing out loud at the irony of my statement!)

I am thought by some to be an expert in autism, but I certainly don't fit *my* idea of an expert. Experts typically have letters after their name, and long lists of universities and not-for-profit organizations on their resumes. Experts, to me, can quote statistics, research studies, and governmental regulations.

Besides, I never sought to be an expert in autism. Which of us does, except for maybe a select few neurologists, psychiatrists, or special education teachers? They probably grew up wanting to be experts in autism. Yet, if you talk to many of these professionals, they will tell you that they never planned on working in the field of autism. Most of us fall into the fold—either by serendipity or by birth.

My boys think I'm an expert in quite a few things—none of which I actually aspired to be expert at! When Spencer was about ten, he outlined his plan for future employment. Our family, he told me, would own and run a zoo. "I'll take care of the reptiles. Joshua can be in charge of the elephants, and all the other mammals that he likes, and Zachary can drive the train!" he said.

"What about Dad?" I asked. "He can be in charge of the gift shop," Spencer replied. "And what will I do?" I inquired. "Well somebody has to cook for us!" (Now why didn't I think of that?)

I have tried, over the years, to attend as many autism conferences and presentations by experts that my budget and life will allow. I love attending the annual Autism Society of America (ASA) conference so that I can soak up the myriad thoughts, research findings, insights, and ideas that are presented there. (I'm proud to say that I've even presented at this conference myself.) Interestingly, when participants register for the ASA conference they are able to choose certain ribbons to add to their badges. The ribbons denote titles such as, *Educator, Chapter Leader, Speaker, Speech-Language Pathologist, Parent*, etc. Everyone walks around with one or two or TEN ribbons hanging from his or her badge. It's a bit comical, actually. I once saw an individual with a ribbon that said, *Somebody*. This visual cue as to who people are got me to thinking about titles. Why couldn't we demarcate the people who *really* are autism experts, so that parents would know whom to talk to and ask questions of? But I know that if I asked some of those I consider to be autism experts, they would refuse to wear a ribbon with the title *Expert*.

I have my own personal cache of experts to whom I turn when I am looking for ideas and answers. I have been highly privileged to meet and talk with Dr. Cathy Pratt, Susan Moreno, Dr. Diane Twachtman-Cullen, Dr. Richard Simpson, Carol Gray, Dr. Catherine Lord, and a host of others whose names I don't have room to list. THEY are experts—not me. They have written books that sit on my nightstand, given presentations that increased my knowledge, and given me insights that have changed the way I interact with my boys. I am still in awe that these amazing individuals know my name. Their expertise has transferred itself to me, and I think I'm getting to the point where I can acknowledge that I, too, am an *expert*.

It's not just an issue of modesty that prevents these individuals from calling themselves experts. It's the realization that the definition of *expert* is not about academic degrees; how many books you've read (or written); or how long you've been in the field of autism. Expertise comes from spending time and emotional energy focusing on the individuals you love and want to support. Expertise comes from an internal drive for insight into the complicated experience we call autism. Expertise comes from days, weeks, months of intervention, trial and error. Expertise comes when you know that you don't have all the answers, but you are willing to ask all the questions.

Surely, that makes every parent an "expert." This new "definition" of *expert* would also include the teacher who toils at night to learn more about autism, the doctor who sees patients on weekends, the speech-language pathologist who spends evenings creating visual systems, and the occupational therapist who spends his or her own money buying more fidget toys. Defining expertise in this light most surely includes the grandparent who stays with his or her grandchild with autism overnight so that the parents can have a well-deserved break. Experts surround us, if only we would broaden our definition to include the wider range of people who care deeply, and make substantial efforts to help.

I have realized that I am an expert in particular forms of autism. Specifically, I'm an expert in Spencer's, Joshua's, and Zachary's autism—how autism feels, looks, and manifests characteristics in their lives. I am an expert in interventions that *support* their individualized needs, and an expert in how to involve them in an activity they don't want to participate in, or structure a meal to include one thing they refuse to eat. And, I am also an expert in how to sleep through the 147th showing of "Shrek"!

Each parent of a child with autism is an expert in his or her own child's "version" of autism. And all of these versions are valid and critical to our cause, whether you have one child with autism or more, and whether you've worked with one child with autism or 10,000. Autism is complex. Treating autism effectively will require experts from every field to share their expertise with each other. As parents, we have the ability to share our expertise on an intimate level by involving ourselves in our child's life and education. Parents also have the ability to encourage all "expert" voices to be heard and valued, whether around the IEP table or the research table. We can use our "expertise" in some way—join a support group, participate in a fundraiser, or loan a good book to a newly diagnosed family.

The critical component of success for our children is the blending of parental and professional expertise. Now I'm off to use my expertise to make dinner!

STRATEGIES FOR BEING AN EXPERT

1. Keep a Record.

Choose a "data collection" method that works for you. Use a journal, calendar with notations, blog, scrapbook, or document file on your computer—something that will allow you to keep notes and thoughts about your child on an ongoing basis. Make notations of changes in behaviors, new language acquired, new self-stimulatory behaviors, doctors' visits, and anything else that seems important at the time. Having this information available during IEP meetings or doctor visits is vital, especially if your child is taking medication for the symptoms of autism.

2. Ask Questions.

Don't hesitate to ask questions of the professionals who surround your child. Questioning is not disagreeing. Asking questions is vital to understanding autism and how it affects your child. Ask questions of other parents of children with autism. Ask questions of your neighbor, your family, and your child's peers. Knowledge is power. And who doesn't want to be empowered?

3. Choose Your Area of Expertise.

It is nearly impossible to be an expert in all the areas of autism. I'm well-versed in most areas of autism, but there are many areas in which I have a basic level of understanding as opposed to "expertise." Anything remotely scientific, such as the DNA impact or neural functioning, leaves my head spinning. I understand the gist of what research scientists discuss in scientific journals, but don't make me quote it! Each parent can choose an area(s) of autism about which they are passionate and become an expert in that area.

4. Understand, and Accept, That Our Knowledge of Autism Is Changing Constantly.

I'm often asked what I think caused autism in my children. I give an answer based upon what I know today. We should all remember that barely 40 years ago, the world believed that autism was caused by really lousy moms who didn't love their children enough. While we are horrified that anyone could have believed that theory, we should remember that in 15 years we may be horrified at the theories we hold today.

PART III

Family Life

CHAPTER 18

Plan A:
Accepting Plan "M"

I once asked Joshua to write the ten things he hates the most. He listed his brother, Zachary, as number one (sigh). Number two? He wrote "Change."

To say that a person with autism doesn't like change is an understatement. The general public doesn't tolerate change well and prefers to have a basic routine to their lives. Vacation from the everyday is great, but most everyone wants to get back to their "usual routine." Individuals with autism spectrum disorders like to have their lives, people, and environments stay the same. Unfortunately, life changes every day. So every single day there are challenges for them to overcome.

Personally Handling Change

I had plans. I was 21 years of age and had my life planned out. I would marry a Californian within five years, have two children, drive a Mercedes, be Vice-President of the home furnishings company that I worked for, and live in a three-bedroom, two-bathroom house on the beach. That was "Plan A."

At the age of 26, I had married a Midwestern hunk, moved to Chicago because of his career, built a home in the suburbs, and discovered that getting pregnant would be nearly impossible for me. Now my plan was to work in downtown Chicago, adopt a child, and find a way to complete my degree in English Literature. I was now working on "Plan C."

Five years later, a developmental pediatrician told us that one of our three sons had autism. We were being presented with "Plan E." One year later, and the diagnosis of autism had been given to our two other sons—we were in "Plan J."

The course of anyone's life rarely turns out to be an exact replica of their initial plans and dreams. I have never met anyone who actually was living "Plan A." And if autism is present in your life? Well, that will guarantee a continual shift and change in your life plans. Whether it's a major change, such as moving to another city or state to access better services for your child, or a minor change, such as turning all music off in the house because your child with autism is sensitive to sound—you can guarantee that there will be a change in your life plan.

The arrival of autism in our life caused a cataclysmic shift in my career plans. We were lucky to be able to make decisions that allowed me to stay home to care for, raise, and work with our boys. While teaching my children, I found my career—my "life's work." I love the challenge of teaching individuals with autism. And I've learned that to live with and teach someone with autism requires that you be more flexible than the person with autism!

Teaching Change

When the boys were young, I understood their need for consistency and arranged our house and our lives accordingly. I had a visual schedule for everything: bedtime, bath time, morning routine, after-school routine, dinnertime, lunchtime, breakfast time, snack time, running errands, going to a friends' house, etc. And the boys thrived on the structure.

I also visually organized their clothing and backpacks. I didn't have much of a choice since boys' clothing doesn't come in a huge variety of colors, and when you have three boys wearing almost the same size, you don't get many options. So I would buy jeans and t-shirts in green, blue, and red. Green was Spencer's favorite color and the only colors left were blue or red, so I chose blue for Josh and red for Zachary. I also labeled all of their closets and drawers with pictures of the items that belonged in the drawers—"pants," "shirts," "underwear," and "socks." I outlined each picture with their corresponding color. I had clothing baskets labeled in their color and taught them to get their corresponding basket of clean clothes, then put the clothes away. I also bought their coats, their backpacks for school, hats, gloves, and anything else they needed in their color code. And they were independent in getting the items they needed because they knew which item was theirs.

I thought I was being very clever and supporting their need for consistency. I had no idea that I had created a routine that would take me years to change. Spencer would wear only green clothing for nearly 12 years. Joshua was 17 before he agreed to wear a black shirt instead of a blue shirt to school. Zachary still insists on wearing a red shirt every single day. No matter what. And Zachary went through a few years when he insisted on wearing the exact same thing that his brothers did. He would sometimes lift up Spencer's shirt and check his underwear to see if Spencer was wearing the blue and yellow striped Fruit-of-the-Loom underwear or the white and gray banded Hanes underwear—because his had to match!

When Spencer was nine, we realized that he needed to wear glasses to see clearly. Spencer and I picked up his glasses from the optometrist, and on the drive home Spencer says, "Mom, Zachary is going to want his own pair of glasses because I have glasses." Oh dear. He was right—Zach would insist on looking EXACTLY like Spencer. Now what do I do?

When we arrived home, Zachary took one look at Spencer and started yelling. Zach ran to Spencer and before I could intervene, he grabbed Spencer's glasses and yanked them off his face, throwing them across the room. Spencer began to yell and cry, Zachary had to be held back from breaking the glasses, Joshua kept asking me what was wrong, and I was attempting to calm everyone down.

My solution? I took an old pair of Craig's glasses, popped out the lenses, and gave them to Zachary. I truly thought that he would put the glasses on and hate the feeling of the plastic around his ears. But no—he liked them. He immediately went to the mirror to look at himself with glasses. Spencer had put his own back on his head and Zach went up to him and smiled. Zachary wore his "glasses" for almost two months, every day. I had to have a few pair of eye glass frames available at all times in case he lost them. The first day Zach wore his glasses to school, I had to explain to his teacher why he was wearing empty eye glass frames. Zachary also hated tears running down his face, so when he was wearing his faux-eyeglasses and would cry, he would stick his fingers through the frames to wipe off his tears. It was hysterically funny!

I tried to put some spontaneity into our lives. I wanted to teach the boys that "change" didn't have to be negative—it could be something wonderful. My first attempt at teaching positive change occurred after the first big snowfall of 2000. There had been a snowfall of about five inches during the school day. This meant that the sledding hills would be pristine. The boys loved to play and sled in the snow, but hated having to wait at the top of the hill for other children to have their turn. So I thought I would surprise them, and take them out of school early to go sledding before everyone else. This would be fun!

I packed up their snow gear, sleds, and snacks and headed to their school. The school secretary called their classrooms and requested that their individual teachers send the boys to the office for an early release. I didn't lie, but I also didn't tell the secretary that I was taking the boys out of school three hours early to go sledding. I think I said that we "had an appointment." Spencer was the first to arrive with an anxious look on his face, almost in tears. "What's wrong Mom? Why are we leaving school? Am I sick?" he said. I told him no, he was fine, he was just leaving school early to go with me somewhere. Joshua arrived, bouncing, jumping up and down and asking me, "What's up Doc? What's up Doc?" Zachary was close on Joshua's heels, grabbing my legs and saying, "Go home? Go home? Go home?"

I ushered the boys out of the school office as quickly as I could and got them outside where I wouldn't feel guilty about telling them that we were going sledding. As I told the boys about our really fun, spontaneous activity the struggle began. Spencer began perseverating (the uncontrollable repetition of a word or action) over having to do his schoolwork later and having too much homework and wouldn't the other kids be angry at him and why would I change the schedule and why didn't I tell them about it in the morning? Joshua just began to cry, saying "no sledding mama! No sledding now!" Zachary started hitting me and threw his boots out the car window. By the time we reached the sledding hill, I had no desire to trudge up and down a snowy hill dragging them on a sled—I wanted to push them down the hill and leave!

I attempted to be spontaneous another time by taking them out of school early to see the midday showing of a new Harry Potter movie. It didn't go well. (See above story.) Once, I decided to have pancakes for dinner instead of breakfast. It didn't go well. (See above story.) And crazy me, I tried to get them to play outside in a warm summer rain storm. The first time didn't go well. (See above story.) The second time it went slightly better. The third time I told them we could play outside in the rain, and went outside myself, splashing around in the puddles and pouring rain without an umbrella and generally making a fool of myself in front of the neighbors—they actually came outside with me! And we had a great time.

Their ability to handle change has increased immensely over the years. I taught "change" in a deliberate format so that they would learn this skill. Teaching, combined with the reality of unexpected change, helped them become much more flexible to the major and minor changes of life. But Zach still wears a red shirt every day!

STRATEGIES FOR DEALING WITH CHANGE

1. Use a "Change" Card.

Teaching change starts with using a visual schedule. Individuals with ASD can't learn "change" if they don't understand the "typical" routine. Once a routine or schedule is followed with minimal stress and/or independently, then it is time to teach change.

I use a visual cue to highlight that change is happening. The visual cue can be almost anything—there isn't any research on what "change" should look like! I believe that the visual cue should be vastly different from anything else they might see so that the message is clear and understandable across environments. I use a fluorescent orange triangle with the word "Change" written underneath it.

2. Teach Positive Change First.

Once a person with autism is comfortable with a routine, change the sequence of tasks by adding a positive activity or reward. For example, if the person is completing a bath time routine independently, put a 'change' card on the schedule and add a preferred treat or activity after the routine is done. Another idea is to change the afternoon homework routine to include a movie. Change the meatloaf you had planned for dinner with their favorite pizza. No matter what positive item or activity that you change, remember to show the person the visual cue of "change." This teaches the person that "change" can be great!

3. Sabotage Consistent Routines.

Handling minor changes to daily life is critical. Using a consistent daily routine, change the sequence of activities and label the rearranged tasks with the "change" card. This could be something as simple as having the person get dressed first before they have breakfast.

Sabotage only one routine a day—you don't want to make the person with autism miserable! And you don't need to change their routines every single day. Just enough that when the inevitable happens, and something needs to change, the person with autism can handle the change with minimal distress.

4. Keep "Change" Cards with You at All Times.

I keep "Change" cards in my purse, my car, my husband's car—anywhere that we might need access to helping the guys cope with change. Even the best-laid plans can be sidelined by the unexpected thunderstorm, a flat tire, changing bedtime, mealtime, or any change in schedule.

CHAPTER 19

Band of Brothers:
Sibling Relationships

1 991. 1992. 1993. The first three years the Chicago Bulls won the NBA Championship with Michael Jordan. It was called "The Three-peat." As in repeat. Times three. Those were also the years our three boys were born. Another "Three-peat"!

We were a family of five before we realized that things about our boys were changing, and not for the better. Our youngest was born before our oldest turned three. We were in the midst of trying to adjust to the demands of having three very young children. I was focused on ensuring that everyone was fed, clean, freshly diapered, and safe—not on their diminishing language, reduced social interactions, and increasing distress. So, all of the boys were with us—and each other—before we knew something was wrong. I tell this only to highlight the fact that the boys have always been together. They don't know a life without brothers. And they don't know a life without autism. Neither do my husband and I.

The Many Faces of Autism

The boys have what I call *conflicting* autism (and that can cause no end of challenges!). One loves to have music playing in the car, another hates it to the point of screaming. One needs to be able to wander around our home at will; another requires ALL doors to be closed and no one to enter his room without knocking. One doesn't like noises, another dislikes silence. One loves SpongeBob, another thinks SpongeBob is a monster of immense proportions. So, as a family, we frequently have to navigate our way through very different autism experiences.

One of our more difficult parental experiences was the boys' sleeping differences. Specifically, they couldn't seem to figure out how to sleep at the same time, so one of them was always awake. Fortunately, however, even when one of the boys was up screaming in the middle of the night, the other two would sleep right through it! Another interesting thing about our boys is that one could be in the midst of a VERY challenging moment AT THE VERY SAME TIME that another would be certain that I really did want to discuss the latest Power Ranger battle!

Like a typical eldest child, Spencer is very protective of his brothers. He has defended Josh in high school, discouraging students who might make fun of him with, "Hey, he's my brother—you gotta love him." Spencer may complain about Zachary and some of his aggressive behaviors, but if anyone else comments on Zach, Spencer is the first one to defend him. This was true even when he was a small child. I once reprimanded Zach for throwing flour all over the kitchen floor, and Spencer was quite upset with me, scolding, "You can't yell at him! He's your best friend!"

Perspectives from inside Autism

It has always been interesting to me to glimpse how the individual with autism perceives his or her life, and in our case with three of the boys on the spectrum, how one brother views another. I got my chance when Spencer was in seventh grade. He was asked to write an essay on something challenging in his life. He chose to write an essay about autism. Below are some excerpts:

> *The way I see autism in Zachary is something that is different [than the way it is] in other individuals. I would describe Zachary's autism as a misunderstanding of how the world around him works. People get autism randomly. You don't know if you'll be born with it or without it. Once you are born, by the time you are about 2 years old, people start to notice that you cannot speak. Autism is not dangerous or deadly, it just makes your life difficult. Autism is also genetic, which means lots of people in a family may have autism. . . .*

> *Autism will last through your entire life. You can't do anything about it, just work with it and make it easier to handle. Treatment and therapies take a lot of work out of the parents. You have to give them some instructions to do things in easier words. The kids also need something to help them talk so other people can understand them. There are lots of different treatments that help with*

listening to music, and working on talking, and learning [how] to act good in public. . . .

Autism has affected my family members because my parents spend a lot of time trying to make my brothers and my life easier and not cause so much trouble. I have a cousin with autism, and my great-uncle had autism, so we have a lot of it in my family. It also affects my family because kids with autism like to go to the same places all the time, like Burger King every day (if mom said yes). And we go to a lot more kid places that maybe are not typical for kids our ages. But my family is trying to make the best of it. . . .

Zachary was just like all the other babies, but I don't remember because I was a little kid too. Mom says that at 18 months of age, Zachary stopped talking, and began being unhappy all the time. He was scared and frightened of everything and yelled a lot, and hit a lot. Zachary is a lot like the guy in [the] "I am Sam" movie only with less words and sometimes less understanding of what people want him to do. But I know Zachary has more intelligence than Sam did in the movie. . . .

I can't answer the last question because I already have a kind of autism called Asperger's Syndrome. So I can't tell you the exact answer. But if you want more information you can ask my mom because she studies autism and we are like her guinea pigs.

As Spencer dictated this essay to me, I was struck by his perception of his life, and that of his brothers. While I was grateful he didn't say his life was horrible (Hooray!), he also thought his life was difficult and that he was a guinea pig (Yikes!). Spencer obviously knew that Zachary was struggling, yet he also knew that his parents were trying to help him and his brothers.

As teenagers, their relationship is quite similar to when they were young—the best of friends, and the worst of enemies all in the same day! They tease each other, laugh with each other, tolerate each other, and, thankfully, love each other.

In this rather "crazy, tragic, sometimes almost magic, awful, beautiful life" we live in (to quote a country music song) I am humbled by the acceptance and love among a rather unusual Band of Brothers.

STRATEGIES FOR DEALING WITH MULTIPLE CHILDREN ON THE SPECTRUM

1. Divide and Conquer.

Craig and I tried to ensure that each boy had some time alone with us. We would have a specific night, once a month, which was Josh's time with Craig, or Spencer's time with me. This allowed them to not feel as if they always had to be together. And we could give our undivided attention to them, even if we were just grocery shopping.

2. Advocate.

Teaching the boys about their autism, and how it was different in each of them, was helpful when they would be frustrated with the others' habits or autism characteristics. If Spencer got really upset because Zach had shredded his favorite green dragon shirt, I could use his understanding of autism to explain why it happened, and how we were trying to change Zach's behavior.

3. Giving Siblings a Script.

Teaching siblings what to say when someone else makes a comment—positive or negative—about their sibling with autism gives them the opportunity to respond appropriately. Many siblings are unsure what to say if they hear someone speaking about their brother or sister. We taught Spencer and Joshua what to say when others' stared at Zachary's pacing, or made comments about his loud noises.

4. Provide Sibling Support.

There are some organizations that provide specific programming and support for siblings of children with autism. These are terrific opportunities for siblings to share thoughts and feelings with other individuals who have experienced the same thing. Everyone needs to know that they are not alone in their struggles—and a sibling event is a great way to do this. If your community doesn't have an event for siblings—make it happen!

5. Allow Frustration and Anger.

Living with a person with autism can be very frustrating—especially if you are sharing a room with them! Allow siblings to be frustrated and/or angry. When taught to express their frustrations openly and appropriately, siblings are less likely to build resentment and distance themselves from the child with autism. Acknowledge that having all your favorite colored pencils snapped in half on the day you need to do an art project is VERY frustrating—but you, as the parent, will help them fix the situation.

CHAPTER 20

Autism Once Removed:
Extended Family Opportunities

When our three boys were diagnosed with autism at the ages of three, two, and one, my parents lived across the country from us. My husband's family lived three states away, and none of our siblings lived nearby. So we lived through the early stages of autism without the benefit of extended family support. We tried our best to describe to members of our family what was happening with our boys, but as we all know, seeing is believing.

The first time my parents and siblings were to see the boys after the onset of their autism was at Christmas time. That year, all of the family gathered at my parents' house for the holiday, including my three brothers and their families. At the time, our combined families totaled 22 people. We tried to explain to family members ahead of time what to expect (and what not to expect) from our anxious, non-verbal, solitary children. My father was quite concerned about the veracity of the boys' diagnoses and asked extensive, probing questions in a phone call prior to the visit. The phone call left me with an uneasy feeling.

I received a letter from my father about a week later. He wrote of his concern that we were getting too caught up in looking for something that wasn't there or justifying bad behavior with a diagnosis. He included a copy of an editorial by Dr. Laura Schlesinger entitled "The Over-diagnosing of America's Children." I was devastated! I couldn't believe that my father didn't believe me—that he thought I could be "making up the autism" to justify ill-mannered children. My hero, my dad, the smartest man in the world, didn't think I knew what I was doing!

All things considered, the Christmas trip went fairly well. We took it upon ourselves to explain to their cousins why the boys wouldn't play with them without some help from adults. We also put a VCR in the room we were staying in, and let the boys "escape" when necessary. While these things did help some, overall the boys didn't sleep well, didn't eat well, and didn't play well. Our family members—though a bit stunned by the intensity level of the challenges—were as supportive as possible.

The next year brought new and difficult challenges. My father had a heart transplant. The year after that, he and my mom moved to the Midwest to live around the corner from us. We were excited to have "Grandma and Baba" living nearby. I was, however, a bit anxious as to how my father would feel about the constant round of therapists, doctors, and educators making trips in and out of our home, especially given his skepticism about the boys' autism. I knew my mom would understand—she always does. But my Dad's potential response worried me.

A week after my parents moved to their new home, I was scheduled to take Zachary to a transition visit at his new preschool. At that time, he was in an autism program at our local preschool, with intensive services to meet his needs. Zachary was really struggling with aggression and anxiety, so I knew that this visit would be difficult. My parents asked to come along and I hesitantly agreed. The visit did not go well. Zach took one look at his classroom, and proceeded to alternately kick, scream, hit, and bite for 20 minutes. He was scared and inconsolable. I was bruised and bleeding. As we left the building, with me carrying a screaming Zach, I glanced briefly at my father. He was crying, and tears were streaming down his face. I asked him if he was all right, and he said, "I had no idea, honey. I am so sorry—I had no idea."

My father had a completely different attitude after that. He was interested and intimately involved in my sons' lives. He would tell others of their autism, and speak proudly of their accomplishments. He would go on walks with Josh, attend school functions with Spencer, and quietly, gently encourage Zach to engage with him. Zachary was particularly difficult with my father. For some reason, every time my father entered our home, Zach would yell at him to "Go away!" Dad would tell him "I love you, Zach" from a distance. It took almost three years before Zach would approach my dad independently (and what a day it was when he did!).

The day that Zach backed into Dad for his "backwards hug" my father broke down and cried, this time with tears of joy. He was their *Baba*—and they loved him as much as he loved them.

Understandably, grandparents and other extended family members sometimes don't greet autism with joy and instant understanding. They are seeing our children "at a distance," not on a daily basis. So the diagnosis of autism may seem like an overreaction on the part of the parents. I've learned that there are different routes to acceptance, some of them more roundabout than others. Some extended family members take more time to acknowledge the presence of autism, while others are quicker to respond. I know that some grandparents get caught up in their fears and worries for their own children, which are very different from those that they have for their grandchildren. In this sense, grandparents mourn twice, once for their children and then again for their grandchildren. I've also learned that gentle teaching, patience, and encouragement can pave the way to acceptance. Acknowledging the ways that grandparents can support their children, and show their love for their grandchildren, can also strengthen family ties.

My father has passed away. He and my mom lived in our home for five years, so my boys were intimately intertwined with their grandfather. They knew of his illness and increasing frailty. My parents were with us through the unbelievably challenging period of Zachary's aggression. I heard (and felt) their prayers on his behalf. I saw and felt the connection that each of my boys had with their grandfather. I also watched them try to cope with the loss of a person they had seen each day and loved. Spencer wears his grandfather's leather coat and Boy Scout ring every day. Joshua repeats to himself through self-talk that Baba was old and nobody lives forever. And Zachary? Well, there are times when Zach is laughing for no reason, looking off into the distance, and I have the feeling that his Baba is giving him a "backwards hug."

Doctor, Lawyer, and Computer Chief: Perspectives from the Uncles

I have three brothers: one older and two younger. I don't have any sisters, which was a source of dismay for me until I turned seven and realized that having a sister would mean sharing a bedroom and clothing! That concept completely changed my mind, and I was very happy to be the only girl! Although there are three years separating each of us, my brothers and I have been exceedingly close, even into our adult years.

I have often wondered if my perspective regarding the impact of my sons' autism on my extended family was the same as my brothers' perspectives. Each of us views family dynamics from a unique vantage point created by our personal histories, emotions, and experiences. I wondered how my brothers viewed their nephews' autism, so I recently asked each of them to share his thoughts with me.

The Doctor: Older Brother Scott

I don't remember the exact moment that I learned about my nephews' autism. I was out of the country for the first few years of their lives, so it wasn't until they were nine, eight, and seven years of age that I really spent time with them. I vividly remember the day I realized that my sister's life was more difficult than I had imagined. Our extended family had come to my town to attend a local festival. Craig, Alyson, and the boys came *specifically* to see the steam locomotive that was on display because of the boys' interest in everything trains. All of us were in the model railroad exhibition tent when Zachary suddenly got upset about something. He started kicking and scratching Alyson, so she took him outside to calm him. Craig was busy trying to help Spencer and Joshua handle the noise of the crowd and the exhibit, so Alyson had to handle Zach on her own. I noticed how scratched, bruised, and scarred her arms were, and realized that this was not the first time Zachary had been aggressive towards her. I was much more sensitive to the challenges of raising three boys with autism after that episode. I also became attuned to how skillfully Craig and Alyson handled their boys, the different roles they performed as mother and father; and how they would "divide and conquer" in order to help all three boys. Most of all, I marveled at how they managed to maintain a sense of humor throughout all of the struggles they had to endure.

There were other lessons learned. My five children have learned that their family relationships may be different with Spencer, Joshua, and Zachary than they are with their other cousins, but also that their relationships with them are no less wonderful, valuable, and loving. They truly love their cousins and enjoy the times they are together. The boys' presence in our lives has taught us to accept people for who they are, see the gifts that differences can bring, and understand that love of family can take many forms.

In my medical practice, I often refer to my sister, Alyson, when I meet patients who have children with autism or who have concerns about their young children.

The Lawyer: Younger Brother Todd

I smile when I think of Zachary and his quotations from movies blurted out to fit the particular situation like, "*That* is so funny. *You* are hilarious!" (from the SpongeBob movie); or the way he would turn his back to me when saying *hi* so that I could hug him from behind. I am always amazed at Joshua's knowledge about trains (to the chagrin of the old men sitting around model train conventions!), and how he used to like drawing Woolly Mammoths mating. As for Spencer, I have told the story about his frustration with church numerous times—specifically, his saying to Alyson, "Jesus, Jesus, Jesus! Why do we *always* talk about Jesus?" I don't seem to remember the difficult times with my nephews. I always remember their talents and enjoy having them in our lives.

Federal Reserve Bank Computer Analyst:
Youngest Brother Reed

I remember the first time that my sister and her family were going to attend a family reunion in California. Weeks before they were to make the trip, she called and asked me to send her my picture so that she could begin to "socialize" the boys to my face so that I wouldn't be a stranger to them when they arrived. I didn't really understand the need for it, but I did it anyway. When the day came and the boys arrived at the house, they became quite agitated because of all the unfamiliar new people. If the truth be told, the boys were really unhappy, "stimming," and generally miserable. Alyson and Craig stepped in and took them to another room where they could be by themselves and calm down. Eventually, after a little time and some interaction with the picture books that Alyson had prepared, the boys were able to tolerate being around all of us. It was this experience that made me want to learn more about my nephews and their autism so that I would know how to make them comfortable, and so they would always know who I was, that I loved them, and would be there for them no matter what their situation.

I'm not sure that I did anything in the intervening years to make things better except that I was around more so that my nephews could become more familiar with me, and I with them. They also grew up, and maturity helped move the process along. It was a mutual thing.

My nephews' autism has really had an impact on my life. Before the boys were diagnosed, I don't believe I had ever known anyone who had autism. Now I notice kids who are struggling more, especially as I travel. I'm not only more forgiving of others with challenges, but also more apt to see their successes, as well. I pay more attention to times when someone might just need a little extra understanding, or when parents may just need to know that someone recognizes that they are doing their best under the circumstances. Interestingly, for some of the people I know, I have become their "mini-expert" whenever they have questions. So I try to stay up to date on the subject of autism. I'm certainly not as knowledgeable as my sister is, but I can always give others her email address!

Helping Extended Family Members Understand Autism

I am very aware of the challenges that many families face in helping relatives to understand and accept their child's autism. Not all family members accept the diagnosis of autism with love and support. Some relatives need extra time to accept the diagnosis and to provide the support that their loved ones need, while others accept, embrace, and enjoy the family member with autism immediately.

My perspective as my boys' mom and my brothers' sister? I am comforted in the knowledge that my boys are loved by their uncles—

not out of duty, but out of shared experiences and their deep appreciation for the gifts that my boys bring into their lives.

STRATEGIES FOR DEALING WITH EXTENDED FAMILY

1. Build Autism Awareness.

If your family will be spending time with extended family members, I highly recommend that you create an opportunity to teach the whole group about autism and how it specifically relates to your child. There are wonderful books that describe autism to children, and other family members. There are also videos that can support your teaching of autism characteristics.

2. Use a Picture Book to Prepare Your Child for Visiting Relatives.

Get pictures of each relative the child may see, and put the pictures into a special book. Review the pictures and names of people prior to a visit, and just before you walk in the door. Pictures of the house they are visiting are also helpful. Even pictures of Grandma's dog will help make meeting new people and faces easier.

3. Manage the Expectations of Others.

Let your family know how you will participate with the larger group, and when you may need to leave. If possible, ask for a specific space that you can retreat to when the noise, crowd, or activity becomes overwhelming. If you let your family know ahead of time that you and your child will not be at Christmas dinner, but will be at the traditional Christmas Eve party, then family feelings don't get hurt when you don't arrive. This includes letting Grandma know that your son isn't going to eat her amazing cranberry sauce, but will eat her mashed potatoes by the plateful!

4. Respond to Criticism with Patience and Understanding.

If a family member criticizes your child for a behavior, or you for decisions you make about your child, try to remember that most negative comments are based on ignorance. I have found that it is better to respond than to ignore. If your brother-in-law says that you should just spank that boy and teach him to mind his elders, you can either poke his eyes out OR you can say, "That's not very helpful. Sam is working very hard to learn to put his shoes on and we are giving him the chance to learn." You may set your brother-in-law on fire in your mind, but not in reality!

CHAPTER 21

Crosswords: Maintaining Your Marriage

Every morning my husband, Craig, and I do the crossword puzzle. Actually, he does the puzzle, and I help out in between making lunches, getting breakfast ready, waking kids up, and signing school papers. It has become our "opening ritual" to start each day. If we get the puzzle done—Hooray! A great day is ahead. These differences in our approach to crossword puzzles mirror our differences in parenting styles.

My husband does a crossword puzzle even if he is out of town. I only do the puzzle when he is around. He enjoys the challenge of the words. I enjoy the interaction with him. For him, it's a mental exercise. For me, it's a social interaction. If we can't figure out a word, Craig works another part of the puzzle, and then returns to the difficult word. If he can't get it, he stops working on the puzzle, perhaps coming back to it at lunchtime. I, on the other hand, can't leave the puzzle until I get it. I look up definitions in our crossword puzzle book, use the electronic crossword-puzzle finder, and ask my mom or dad for help. I will even look up definitions on the internet. I search out every resource possible to find the answer that I need. Craig relies upon his own knowledge, circling the problem from all angles until the whole puzzle makes sense, and then the word (usually) comes to him.

When the boys were young and newly diagnosed, I was unrelenting in my need for information. I would pounce upon strangers on the street if I thought that they might possibly know something about autism. I read books, hunted out websites, talked to people, toured schools, and basically "inhaled" any and all information I could obtain. When Craig didn't do the same, I spent a lot of wasted time resenting him for what I perceived to be his abdication of parental responsibility. How could he *not* want to read the latest research? How could he know how to be a good parent for our guys if he didn't attend a conference?

It took a few years, and a bit of marriage counseling, for me to acknowledge and recognize that his parenting style was just as vital to my children's growth and progress as my own. Both of us made mistakes along the way, but each of us learned what we needed to know in our own learning styles. Thankfully, both of us learned to accept the value of different parenting interactions. Most importantly, we accepted that although we might parent differently, both of us love our boys deeply.

I had much to learn about how to be a good parent AND still be a good companion to my husband. Our meetings with a marriage counselor were quite eye opening for me. One evening, Craig told the counselor that he was deeply jealous of the time I gave to our children, and deeply angry at himself for being jealous of his own children. I realized that if I wanted to maintain my marriage, I would need to be a better partner to my husband, not just a good therapist to my children—almost a more difficult task than coordinating an ABA program!

During the Christmas holidays of 2005, my mother became very ill and circumstances required that I stay at home with her and my father while my husband took the boys on our planned and pre-paid vacation. He took them to San Diego, California for a week. I know that he was a bit hesitant, and I was more than a bit concerned as to how he would handle the boys alone, but he bravely got on an airplane with them and headed to the West Coast. On the day the "troop" went to the Wild Animal Park, Spencer called me on my cell phone to tell me how the day trip was going. He described all of the animals he had seen, the things his brothers had done wrong, and then told me that there was a great hot air balloon ride that would allow you to fly over the top of the park and see all the animals—but his Dad had said it was too expensive. My parents, upon hearing this while in the hospital room, told Spencer that they wanted to pay for the balloon ride. The boys were thrilled and told their Dad.

About 45 minutes later I got a call from Craig. He said to me, "I'll describe the balloon ride for you. There is a big yellow balloon and this basket . . ." Eventually, he said to me, "The balloon is about 300 feet up in the air now. The boys are having a great time. Oh, now I can see it's up to about 400 feet."

I did a double take at his words.

"Craig, honey, where are *you*?"

"You know how I feel about heights," said Craig. "I'm on the ground."

I could not believe it. My husband had sent my three sons WITH AUTISM up in a hot air balloon by themselves, and I was nearly across the country! Of course, I also realized that Craig hadn't been concerned about the cost of the ride at all! He just didn't want to go up in the balloon with the boys. I nearly came unglued and if I could have lunged through the phone I would have.

Fortunately, I realized that I was the one with the problem. My boys loved their adventure! They took the video camera up with them, and videotaped the whole ride for me to see. They were confident, fearless, and proud of their cool ride in the hot air balloon. If I had been there, I would not have seen this experience as an opportunity for independence. Craig did.

Parenting differences can sometimes cause problems for our consistency-needing kids with ASD. But the differences can also provide them with opportunities for exploration, and for handling different kinds of people and situations. Craig handles the boys' autism by experience and by trial and error. I handle their autism by researching and reading. He believes in trial by fire. I believe in discrete trial! Our boys have benefited from both of our styles, and our marriage has benefited by our acceptance of both styles. We've said a few *cross words* along the way. But the "words" of our parenting crossword have meshed and overlapped nicely to complete the puzzle of our lives.

STRATEGIES FOR KEEPING YOUR MARRIAGE STRONG

Craig and I have had the opportunity to do presentations on keeping your marriage together when you have children with autism. We consider this experience an immense privilege. We also want to be clear that we do not have all the answers—just our own experience. The following strategies are from both of our perspectives and are intended for both partners.

1. "Different" Does Not Mean "Wrong."

Handling a situation differently than the other spouse does not mean it was handled incorrectly. If the outcome was positive, keep your mouth closed! If the outcome was not positive, wait until everyone is calm before discussing how to approach the same situation in another manner.

2. Take Time to Be Together.

We have a strong belief in babysitters! We tried to get out of the house together at least once a month. We paid a higher rate than any other family in the neighborhood just to ensure loyalty! We initially went out for just a half-hour, then as the boys got used to the babysitter, we expanded our time out together. Even if we had dinner out, or just ran errands, we were able to leave our parent-selves at the door.

3. A Night Away Keeps Divorce at Bay!

We know that there are parents who will say, "There is no possible way I can leave my child overnight." They are wrong. You can do it, and you should. If possible, try to get two nights away each year. You'll be amazed at how much more solid your marriage will be, when you have some time to be together as a couple—not as the parents of a child with autism.

4. Hobbies Are Important.

We recognize that each of us needs time alone to be an individual. We try to support each other in our respective hobbies (passions, obsessions—whatever you want to call them) so that we are not defined solely by autism and our children. Taking time to shift your thinking and brain cells to a favorite activity will really give you more energy for thinking about autism—and ensuring that your spouse gets that opportunity is a guarantee that he or she will ensure you get an opportunity also!

CHAPTER 22

Conflicted and Coming to Terms: Aggression,
Self-Injury, and Other Difficulties

I am known in most circles as the mom with a funny story or cheerful insight into parenting kids with autism. And that has been true until recently. And I *will* tell amusing anecdotes again soon—but not at this time. I'm committed to being honest with anyone who asks, however painful it may be, and I am passionate about everyone in the world of autism sharing their stories with each other, no matter how messy or conflicted they are.

Our family has been living in a yawning canyon of challenge and anguish for quite some time now. Through it all, I have tried to focus on the positives, but there are times when this is very difficult to do. This is one of those times. Since our darling son, Zachary, was struck by the anvil of puberty, he has become a different person—and not a happy one. Our once cheerful, smiling, dimpled, non-verbal son has become a terribly unhappy, angry young man.

Zach has always had a fight-or-flight response to anxiety—usually *both* fight and flight. When he was young, I sported quite a few bruises, bites, black eyes, and unsightly scratches. I've had my share of well-meaning neighbors, doctors, and total strangers query me about my relationship with my husband when they saw the marks. How do you explain to someone that it's your four-year-old who has caused you to look like an eggplant? I learned how to restrain Zach in order to protect myself and others. I was appalled that I needed to know how to defend myself against a child that I loved.

Our response to all of this? We worked on behavior, counseled with doctors on medication, changed his environment, and ultimately found success. The violence diminished greatly, so much so that it became a non-issue. For six years, Zach was the child we had hoped he could be—challenged with autism, yes, but wonderful to raise. Then puberty hit!

Zach's downward spiral has been accompanied by violent, aggressive episodes. Because these episodes are triggered by so many things, it has not been possible to keep track of what the antecedents are. We can, however, keep track of the frequency. "Good" days have one or two violent episodes. Bad days? Six or more, and someone is inevitably bleeding. For a while, we could actually see the cycle of violence coming. First Zach would squeeze your wrist, then start yelling, then hit you on the shoulder, then escalate to hair-pulling, biting, and screaming. His eyes would glaze over, and a blank expression would cross his face. At that point he would "leave us," and it could sometimes take more than 30 minutes for him to "come back."

We knew the episode was over when he would burst into tears, and look around, almost puzzled, saying "Sorry. Sorry Mama."

Zach seems as powerless as we are to control or predict his rages. I've tried everything I can think of. I've changed his curriculum, modified his diet, increased his sensory interventions, documented his behavior on numerous charts, talked to four doctors in as many different states, and asked advice from every expert I know. Nothing has significantly changed. It is true that regression on the part of the child causes regression on the part of the parent. Zach's regression into violence has moved my family and me back to an emotional state of weariness, exhaustion, and frustration. When none of the interventions we try contribute to improvement, we feel incompetent and embarrassed by our inability to understand him and to provide what he needs.

When my parents lived with us, I was constantly worried that one or the other would get a broken bone, or something more horrible, if they tried to step in and help during an episode.

Ninety percent of the time, the violence is directed at me. Based on my experience with Zach, I think I know a bit of what it must feel like to be a victim of abuse, although I know that there is no willfulness or volition in his behavior. Still, I carry with me physical and emotional scars. I tense up and flinch sometimes when he walks up to me, even as I vehemently defend Zach's behavior to others, and refuse to listen to *any* negative talk about him from others. And yes, there are those days when it takes every bit of willpower I have not to yell at him to STOP.

One of these rage episodes happened while I was driving. The boys and I were heading home from school. Zach was in the front seat. All of a sudden, he started yelling, and before I could pull over, he grabbed my hair, and yanked my head down. I did finally make it to the side of the road, and got both of us out of the car. He continued to attack me, and while I was attempting to keep him from hurting both of us, a state trooper happened to drive past. He stopped and approached Zach. While the ensuing interaction is a painful memory of flashing images, I will never be able to delete from my mind the overriding image of my son lying on the ground while a policeman held him down and handcuffed him to prevent him from attacking me. I also have another vivid picture in my memory—one of a vastly different time and place—a starkly contrasting image of Zach winking at me, kissing me on the arm, and saying "You're cute!" How do I resolve these conflicting images?

Not long ago, our oldest son, Spencer, came into my room and lay down on my bed with his head in his arms. His expression was desolate. When I asked him what was wrong, he told me that he has nightmares. I launched into my mom-speech about nightmares-are-just-imagination, when he stopped me and said," But Mom, I constantly dream that Zach kills you."

Our second son, Joshua, struggles to go to sleep because he's afraid that Zach will get up in the middle of the night and hurt me. He paces the hallway outside my room for more than an hour after he is supposed to be in bed, asking me if I'm sure I'll be okay.

My husband's job requires him to frequently travel. He calls me incessantly while he is gone, worried that I am hurt. The stress and worry of not being able to be at home to support me is overwhelming for him.

My family and I have found a private residential school that we believe can help Zach. The decision to send him away from us is so painful that I can barely think it, let alone write it. I'm inexorably conflicted about our decision. *How can it possibly be right to have him live away from the people who love him unconditionally? How is it possible that I can't find a better answer?* We didn't make this decision lightly, of course. And I probably wouldn't have supported it, if it weren't for my other boys.

So, I am constantly conflicted in knowing what is right, and whom to support. Why does it feel like I'm choosing between my family members? I also feel guilty over not making a decision sooner. I kept thinking that I should be able to handle this—I'm an AUTISM consultant for heaven's sake! And I have a parent's near-constant optimism that tomorrow will be better. But the longest we've gone this year without a violent episode is ten days. Our whole family is frustrated, desperate, and so very, very tired.

I do realize now that I cannot help Zach by myself. I have thought long and hard about what it would take to help him at this point. And I think it would take three people, 24 hours a day, seven days a week, to maintain a schedule, place logical, everyday demands on him, and deal with the behavior that will surely stem from those demands. That kind of support isn't available within my home.

I broke down the other night while helping Zach into bed. I was overwhelmed at the thought that no one would tuck him in, and whisper our bedtime mantra to him—"Good night. Sweet Dreams. I love you. See you in the morning." I've researched the school we selected thoroughly, and know that the people who work there are kind and generous people. *But they aren't me. So how can it be better?* Conflict arises once again, as I ponder whether my resistance to having him leave us is based upon my own insecurities, instead of thinking about what is best for him. How do I separate the two? *Right now, I don't know which causes greater stress—living with Zach, or living without him.*

For Christmas, my husband gave me a series of creative gift certificates. One promised me a major construction project within our home. Another granted me a weekend away with my girlfriend, and another was for a foot massage. The most telling certificate was for a "No Zach Day." I burst into tears while reading it. *It seems horrible to be so happy about a day away from the child I adore.* Conflicted, yet again!

I don't know if I will ever find a peaceful resolution to my conflict. My cerebral, consultant-self knows that our decision is sound, and should be viewed as another intervention—not a lifetime commitment. But my emotional, mom-self screams that it can't possibly be right. This "self" causes me to ask myself painful questions. Is it my pride talking, or is it a mother's intuition? Do I selfishly want Zach at home to make me feel better, or will my concerns be justified by his spiraling out of control even more?

After months of wading through the molasses-like morass of government and educational paperwork, we were finally given a date on which to enroll Zach in his new school. I haven't stopped crying since I read the letter.

I know that some of you have made this same very painful decision, and have felt as conflicted as I do. At least, I'm hoping that some of you feel this way. I don't want to know if I'm the only one to feel as I do. Truly, the only solace I feel at this time comes when I realize that others have done this before me, and have found help and improvement in the midst of difficult decisions. It is comforting for me to know that I am not alone. And I hope, now, that some of you will know it also, and find comfort in the knowledge.

We enrolled Zachary in January of 2007. Since then, many families have shared their own stories of difficult decisions, and their support and concern for my family and me. We are forever grateful for that support. The writing below chronicles our journey from his enrollment until April 2010.

Three years, three months, two days, seven hours and 18 minutes. That's how long it has been since we enrolled Zachary in a residential school for children with autism and significant behavioral challenges. The decision to do so was gut-wrenching; the weeks following his enrollment, traumatizing.

In the first six months after Zach started school, my husband and I didn't know what to do with ourselves. Our lives had changed drastically. Without the constant need to supervise Zachary we were lost, at times wandering about the house, wondering what we were supposed to do with our time. Those first six months took their toll on Zach, as well. He lost weight, broke out in eczema, and struggled to sleep. *We felt his absence keenly.*

There were moments of shock and clarity at how different my life was without Zachary needing me every minute of every day. I started keeping a list of the changes in my life as I floundered, trying to understand this new routine. The list of the drastic changes in my life follows, in the order I noticed each of the differences:

- I can have the TV on while I'm getting ready in the morning.
- I talked to a friend on the phone for more than a minute.
- I don't carry my cell phone with me everywhere I go.

- I slept through the night.
- No one yelled at me this morning.
- I had threads hanging on the cuff of my pants—no one noticed or tried to cut them off.
- I cooked breakfast and was able to clean the dishes immediately.
- I went to Target and didn't buy a train.
- I slept through the night for two days straight.
- No one has said the word *HAPPY* to me in eight days.
- I haven't been kissed by one of my boys since Zach left.
- I haven't cried in 36 hours.
- I actually went to bed at 9:00 p.m.—just because I was tired.
- I finished a scrapbook project.
- I worked a full day and there wasn't a crisis at home that required me to leave work.
- Josh hasn't yelled in two weeks.
- My house is silent.
- I'm alone more than I've ever been.
- No one waits outside the shower for me, pacing and vocalizing.
- I soaked in a tub-bath uninterrupted.
- I don't have any bruises, bite marks, scratches, or cuts.
- I haven't been inside a Burger King in 28 days.
- I went overnight to a spa with my sister-in-law, and I didn't call home for 24 hours.
- I actually laughed out loud today.
- I felt like I was forgetting something all day long—then realized that it was Zach.
- I started crying for no reason.
- I haven't spoken to our pediatrician in a month.

- I realized that I was happy today. Then felt guilty that I was.
- I woke at 4:00 a.m., tears streaming down my face, and hearing my brain scream, *"I want Zachary home."*

It took six months for all of us to adjust. As for Zachary, he never cried or got upset when we left his school after a visit. We knew that this meant he was doing all right, because he has *always* been extremely capable of telling us when he doesn't like something! The staff was wonderful to him, and to us, as we made the difficult adjustment to a life lived separately. I felt somewhat better about our decision when we got a phone call from Zach's house manager about a month into his enrollment. He said that Zach had been unhappy that evening, and he thought that Zach was homesick. I was touched and reassured by the recognition that, beyond his autism, Zach was a young man who missed his family.

In three years, the whole family has changed—and it's been a positive change. My other two sons are calmer, and have enjoyed having me available to attend school events and karate demonstrations. My husband and I have adjusted to not being in a constant state of stress and worry. We actually have a little bit of time to pursue our hobbies. I've even been able to expand my work with other individuals with autism. And Zachary? He's a much happier guy than he has been in years.

We visit Zach every two to three weeks. We talk with him every week via internet camera. He's been home for vacations, holidays, and weekend visits. In three years, we've had only three aggressive incidents when he has been home, and even those moments were minimally challenging, compared to the prior violent episodes before he left. He has gained two grade levels academically, grown to a towering 6'3", and now eats almost everything he sees. He even sang and danced in a school performance!

There are still times when I miss him so terribly that I want to hop in the car and bring him home. Even though I know that he is content and learning at school, I still struggle to leave him after a visit. The conflicted emotions that I had at the beginning of this journey still exist. But I now know that those emotions are more about my missing Zach than worrying whether we have made the right decision. Our decision was right—for me, my other sons, my husband, and for Zachary—maybe not the right decision for other families, and definitely not a decision I ever wanted to make, but it was right for us.

It seems to me that everything in life has a positive and negative side. Autism, as a diagnosis, is a both a challenge and a gift. Our children can bring the greatest joy and the greatest sorrow to our lives. Parents of children with autism know that decisions regarding therapies, treatments, and interventions all come with opposing viewpoints. In fact, there isn't any decision we make for our children that isn't fraught with a "yin-yang effect."

I have heard many parents lament the decisions they have made for their children as they walk the path of autism. The self-recrimination typically starts with, "I wish I had," and usually ends with, "Do you think it would have made a difference?" The answer to that question can never be known. So, I have stopped worrying and perseverating over a path not taken or past decisions that cannot be changed. Instead, I try to focus on making the best decisions for my family and myself for the future.

I have learned to accept that regardless of "super mom" aspirations, I really am human (stunning isn't it?), and as such, I may make the wrong choice sometimes. But the decision to get additional help for Zachary, at a critical juncture in his life, wasn't one of them. Clearly, this has been the right choice for him and for our family. Zach needed (and wanted) to have an environment that could teach him how to be happy again, to be his dimpled, cheerful self. He has been successful in that endeavor and has also learned many new things. We, too, have achieved a kind of success. We have learned to live with an empty bedroom, even as we rejoice in Zachary's progress.

**For those families interested, Zachary is enrolled in Chileda Institute, in LaCrosse, Wisconsin. You can find out more at www.chileda.org.

STRATEGIES FOR DEALING WITH DIFFICULT DECISIONS

1. Be Selective in Asking for Opinions.

Any time we make a decision—whether choosing an intervention, a school, an IEP goal, or choosing a physician—everyone you speak to will have an opinion. Making decisions using the majority opinion may not provide the best answer for your specific child and situation. Go to your most trusted supporters for advice.

2. Trust Your Intuition.

Parents know their child better than anyone, but frequently dismiss their own feelings when making decisions. Even if you have never read a single book on autism, you still have intuitive knowledge of what your child needs.

3. Practice Full Disclosure.

Many parents refuse to tell others that certain behaviors have become unmanageable. Some are fearful that they will be ridiculed, or thought incompetent. Some worry that telling a teacher or therapist that their child has significant physical aggression will start a spiral of government interference. However, sharing the clear facts and reality of aggression with others provides access to services and supports, and allows parents to stay in control. If aggressive behaviors are not addressed, they will escalate and the decision of how to handle the behaviors may be taken out of the parents' hands.

4. Stop Second-Guessing.

All parents make the best decisions that they can, with the information they have at the time, and given their specific family dynamic. Looking backward and regretting a particular decision is helpful only if using "hindsight" allows for better decisions in the future. Worrying over whether a decision should or shouldn't have been made three years ago won't accomplish anything.

5. Separate Emotion from Fact.

It is difficult for parents to put aside our emotional connection to our children in order to make a "logical" decision. Writing down the benefits versus the detriments of a decision can help. Then give the list to a trusted friend or advisor to get an objective viewpoint of the positive and negatives.

CHAPTER 23

Odd Mom Out:
Life Outside the Norm

In 1991, I was a surprised, ecstatic mom of a lovely baby boy. In 1992, I was a surprised, but cheerful mom of two darling boys. In 1993, I was a shocked, but happy, sleep-deprived mom of three boys under the age of three. In 1994, I was an overwhelmed, frantic, determined-to-be-optimistic mother of three boys with autism. Yet, I still saw myself as a typical, suburban mom with a little house, little van, little children and little sanity. I was wrong—*typical,* I wasn't!

My husband encouraged me to join the young mother's group at our church so that I could get out of the house once a month. My first night at group began to peel away my notions of typicality, as I listened to these moms swap stories of toilet training, playgrounds, and places to get a good deal on children's clothes. My head was spinning with

189

questions about therapies, eating issues, and sleeping. One conversation in particular, clearly showed me that I was no ordinary mom. The women were complaining to each other about the constant whine of their children's voices as they called "Mom" throughout the day. They laughed and joked about how their heads hurt from the constant verbal banter and they wished that their kids would just be quiet for ten minutes. I started to cry, and left the building.

I couldn't even relate to these women's "issues." All I wanted was to hear a single word out of one of my sons' mouths. I would have done anything to hear them say "Mom," but I would have been satisfied with far less—with words like, "go," "drink," or "hungry." Anything! I knew then that I would not ever be an ordinary mom, because I could never relate to any of the typical "mommy frustrations." Each step toward development was far too precious to me. Each glance, each hug, each sound that my boys made set me apart from other moms because I reveled in those milestones, and I lived off those small steps forward for months.

Each foray into the typical suburban life demonstrated again and again, how "odd" my parental experience really was. For example, the boys took swimming lessons at our local YMCA when they were five, four, and three. While the other moms sat and chatted, poolside, swapping decorating ideas and "war stories," I was in the pool helping the instructor teach my boys how to swim using visuals. While other moms and dads sat in the stands at Little League games yelling at the umpire, I was my son's team coach so that he could participate. Other moms drove their kids to ballet, basketball, and bassoon lessons. I drove to therapy, therapy, and more therapy!

Ordinary parents spend their money on Nike shoes and savings for college. We spend our money on applied behavioral analysis. Typical families go on vacation. We go to autism conferences. Typical parents read report cards. We read Individual Education Plans (IEPs) that are 40 pages long, and require us to sit for hours in meetings discussing services and interventions. Typical families go to movies together. We . . . oh wait! We DO go to movies together. Does that make us ordinary?

I knew I had to find a place where I would not be the "odd mom out." So, I went to an autism support group in our area, and like that first church group I attended, these parents also discussed their children's issues. The difference was that they discussed the issues that I was concerned about—communication, sensory integration, and behavior. When I introduced myself to the group I described my three sons with autism and talked about their specific diagnoses. I also made some humorous comment about the crazy life we were leading. The president of the support group looked at me, and said sarcastically, "You are *way* too happy. You're going to end up on medication if you don't start to deal in reality." Could it be that typicality was eluding me again simply because I was determined to be optimistic?

I wondered if there would ever be a place where I could connect to other moms and not feel like the "odd mom out." Over a few years, and a few moves to other cities, I did find quite a few individual moms whose "oddness" matched mine. And I eventually started an autism support group in a city that didn't have one, so that I could surround myself with wonderful, fantastically odd moms. I envisioned myself, once again, as a "typical" mom. And, once again, I was wrong.

There are periods of time when I feel that our family is doing really well—when I think we are probably just like every other family in our community. We're dealing with homework, school, dinner, and chores. It all seems so typical. And then we venture out of our home to a local area, like the park, or a restaurant. And our uniqueness—our oddness, our autism—is glaringly obvious.

I remember times during the summer months when I would sit in the front yard watching over and playing with my boys. They love water, so one of their favorite activities was to fill buckets up with water, and run the hose over the driveway to cool the cement so that they could enjoy the splash and sparkle of shooting water in the sunlight. I noticed other children outside, playing games together and running around the neighborhood. But I never saw another mom sitting outside, directing their children's play. They seemed not to worry about their children's whereabouts, fearing that they would bolt into the street or wander off to watch a bee fly into the neighbor's yard. Where were all those other moms? What did they do with their days, if they didn't spend their time hovering over their children, prepared and ready for any number of interesting, and potentially dangerous scenarios? What do typical moms do in the summer days of no school and lovely weather? The oddness of my experience was again causing me to stand out in the crowd.

The boys are teenagers now, and over the years I've come to terms with my "a-typicality." Nevertheless, I still have moments when it's glaringly obvious that I will never be a typical mom. Our oldest son joined the swim team last year, with much encouragement on our part, and significant anxiety on his part. It was a wonderful experience. He's on the team this year too, and we are so very proud of him. He went to the team dinners before the swim meets, even though he wouldn't eat any of the food that was served. He does the team cheer with the group, even though the cheer is quite loud and consists of gibberish that only teenage boys can find invigorating. Sometimes, he even jokes with the other swimmers. My goal was for him to participate. I didn't, and still don't, care if he is the best swimmer on the team. (Just don't let him be the worst!) We have enjoyed going to his meets, cheering him on, and hosting the team for breakfast or dinner.

But at the closing banquet, a video was played showing casual snapshots of the team throughout the season. Not a single picture of my son was in the video. I heard all of the other parents and swimmers joking and laughing about each of the photos, and truly, it was fun to see. I listened while the coaches and parents discussed which awards were won, who had the best time, and which swimmer was the most spirited. Our son's accomplishments were not among them. Our priorities were not the priorities of others in the room. In fact, I would bet that it had never occurred to any of those parents to worry about their sons' willingness to say hello to another person, let alone winning the 400-meter freestyle. But I knew that Spencer had achieved his own goal of joining a sport team, and being part of a group.

Our definition of success will always be different from that of other parents. We will never be typical parents, and I will always be the "odd mom" out. I am really comfortable with my oddness on most days. I am generally happy with our uniqueness as a family. I love the quote from Liane Holliday-Wiley in her book, *Pretending to be Normal*: "We have a picture of family that others consider odd and unusual. But it's our picture—and it's perfect."

I still have moments when I think, "I'll bet other moms don't have to worry about this." Like the email I got from Josh's teacher the other day. It read: "The library ladies would appreciate it if Josh didn't use their Kleenex to wipe his sweaty armpits. Please talk to him about this."

I laughed for quite a while. And then went upstairs to have another "odd mom out" moment and talk to Josh about the true purpose of Kleenex tissues!

STRATEGIES FOR LIVING A "NORMAL" LIFE

1. Volunteer in Your Community.

Whenever possible, find a way to volunteer in your community. Being part of your community, even in a small way, allows you to feel part of a larger group. And you get to spread the word about autism.

2. Social Media Can Provide Perspective.

The prevalence of internet, email, Facebook, blogs, and chat rooms has greatly improved the ability to connect with others who share our interests and priorities. Sharing in these connections can help when you think you are the only mom, or dad, who has ever washed the same shirt every night for the past year because your child wouldn't wear any other shirt.

CHAPTER 24

'Tis the Season: Holidays

I f there were an "Alcoholics Anonymous" type of group for holiday fanatics, I would be a lifetime member! It takes me two full days to decorate for Halloween, and Thanksgiving dinner is just the intervening meal I eat before starting to decorate for Christmas! My house at Christmas can make Rockefeller Center in New York City look positively stark. As soon as the holiday season rolls around, I start planning, and my boys start rolling their eyes and muttering about hauling Rubbermaid™ containers filled with decorations up and down the basement stairs.

Many people marvel at the way my boys with autism handle the constant changes in décor that occur in our home. I think they're just so used to the changing "holiday landscape" that they don't realize that other people who celebrate Christmas typically decorate only one as opposed to four trees! Actually, they're probably baffled that other people don't have mummies on their front porches during the month of October.

Halloween is one of my favorite holidays. There's something about the gruesome, dark attitude of celebrating monsters and ghosts that enables me to shed my cheerful, optimistic self and embrace a darker, slightly-out-of-whack persona. In October, you'll find me mumbling in *Rainman* fashion, "Skulls. Definitely Skulls." Halloween is also one of my kids' favorite holidays because it equates to a night of sugar! Trick-or-treating was one of the first discrete trial ABA lessons my kids learned. It's a quick "cause and effect" lesson—knock on a door, say *Trick or Treat* (or nothing at all, which also works), and a total stranger will give you candy. Zach was highly resistant to this concept at first, refusing to approach the door, limply dropping to the sidewalk, and screaming at the top of his lungs. We manually "guided" him up to the first friendly, accommodating neighbor, and the minute she dropped a piece of candy in that goody bag—BANG! His eyes lit up; he looked at us with an expression of bafflement and wonder; and off he went, quick as a rabbit, to the next house. Of course, when he kept leaving our house for the next five days, running around the neighborhood ringing doorbells, we knew we had created a real Halloween monster!

The costumes at Halloween also provide plenty of learning opportunities. Not for us, mind you—but for our friends and neighbors. My boys tend to choose rather unusual characters for costumes. Not the typical Spiderman, prince, clown or ghost for us! As a kindergartner, Spencer was adamant about being The Black Fox from the old Danny Kaye movie, *The Court Jester*. When no one in the whole school knew who he was supposed to be, he burst into tears. In second grade, Josh wanted to be Dexter from the cartoon *Dexter's Laboratory*, and ended up actually looking like a loony bin escapee! Throughout the years, one or the other boy has been a Viking, Bullwinkle, a lobster, Simba, a confederate army general, a Pokemon master, a knight (with chain mail), and a Circus Ringmaster.

Unlike Halloween, Thanksgiving is a very stressful holiday in our home. How could it not be? It's a holiday centered on foods that my guys won't eat! One year, we had four other families join us for Thanksgiving, since they, like us, didn't have family nearby with whom to celebrate. That meant we had eight adults, and 29 children for Thanksgiving dinner! We set up games and activities for the kids, and served them a fabulous Thanksgiving meal. After the adults got the kids settled in with plates, we sat down to eat at the "adult" table. A short time later, I got up to see how my boys were handling the meal, but didn't find them at the table. I started looking in other rooms, the basement, outside—no Beytien boys. Then I walked past the pantry, and saw a light coming from underneath the door. When I opened the door, I found my three boys sitting on the floor of the pantry passing around a box of Lucky Charms cereal. So much for that great Thanksgiving meal! Somehow, those delicious yams had escaped my boys' attention.

And, of course, there is the joy of Christmas—my favorite holiday. I love the décor, the music, the cheer—in fact, just everything about it! My kids have grown up with my "over the top" Christmas attitude, so they aren't fazed by the four trees, the garland, the lights, or the other accoutrements that make the holiday special. But the giving of presents? Now, that's where the challenges begin.

Josh can't stand the anxiety of waiting to find out what he's going to get for Christmas. So, sometime in October, he begins to make a list of what he wants. His list includes not only the items he wants, but also the websites where you can buy them, their prices, and a small drawn box at the end of each line that provides a space for us to initial which item we will be purchasing. Josh then passes his list around to those who he knows will buy him gifts so that they can "register" his presents. On Christmas morning he will open his gifts and truthfully say, "Thanks! It's just what I wanted!"

Two years ago, we decided that it was time for the boys to purchase gifts themselves for other people in the family. So we put all of our family names into a bowl, and had each family member choose the name of a person to buy a gift for. My father got Josh's name, and Josh quickly asked him "What are you going to buy me?" My dad suggested to Josh that he make a list of five things that he wanted, explaining that he would choose one of those items as Josh's gift. Josh thought for a minute and said, "How about if I list four and you buy them all?"

Coincidentally, Josh had picked his grandfather's name from the bowl. I prompted him with the question, "What do you think Grandpa will want for Christmas?" He paced back and forth, with one hand behind his back, and a finger tapping his forehead muttering, "Think. Think. Think." He whipped around, finger in the air, and said, "I know! Pills! Grandpa loves pills!" My father is a heart transplant recipient, so he takes a handful of pills two or three times a day. Josh's response was entirely logical, even if atypical.

Although the settings of our holiday gatherings may be wild, the actual celebrations themselves are rooted in the needs of our children.

We may have a single party, but the numbers are limited, and the boys are allowed to "escape" to their rooms, as needed. Extended family may join us for a meal, but the boys are only expected to sit with us for a few minutes. I also allow them to eat foods they really want on these occasions. My priority is for them to enjoy the presence of family and friends, so I don't worry about issues that might concern me on another day—such as whether the meal includes anything nutritious! Christmas Day is a very calm, easy-going day for us. We maintain routines, eat breakfast, open a few gifts, and immerse ourselves in trains, Anime, and Discovery channel DVDs. We indulge the boys' passions by giving them gifts that encompass their intense interests. And, we celebrate those passions with our boys as we rejoice in the time we spend with one another.

STRATEGIES FOR HOLIDAY HAPPINESS

1. Use Visuals.

- If you're traveling, put together a book with pictures of where you're going, and of the people you will see.
- Create a "schedule" of the holiday events, especially when the event will be over!
- Include a visual of an activity that the child will enjoy, or a picture in the schedule of their "alone time" so that they know they will be getting a break at some point.

2. Provide Solitude.

- Designate an area just for your child. If the gathering is at your home, then calmly tell others that your child's room is his or her safe haven.
- If you are at another's home, ask if there is a room that can be used for this purpose. Bring favorite toys, movies, etc., to put in the room. If this is not possible, there's always a drive in the car!

3. Keep a Schedule.

Do everything you can to maintain your child's routine. Even on Christmas Day, Hanukah nights, or whichever holiday you celebrate, keep the child's schedule as consistent as possible.

4. Promote Awareness.

Some of the greatest advocacy moments come when you promote autism awareness with your extended family. If you aren't comfortable "presenting" to the aunts, uncles, and cousins some basic info on autism, consider using the "Souls: Beneath and Beyond Autism" DVD or a book written for children to spark a conversation. Give autism t-shirts, jewelry, and books as gifts. After all, every bit of knowledge your family gains will provide more support to you and your child throughout the year.

CHAPTER 25

The Trip:
Traveling with Autism

T he expressions on people's faces ranged from mild curiosity to
incredulousness.

"You're going where?"

"Waco, Texas," I replied.

"Why?!"

The answer to that question was simple *if* you know my son, Josh.
We were going to Waco because Joshua was turning 16. Because
Joshua has always been passionately interested in large mammals.
Because we have friends whose daughter is the large mammal
zookeeper at the Cameron Park Zoo and she had offered for Josh
to come to Waco and be "zookeeper-for-the-day." Because I had
no idea what to get my 16-year-old son for his birthday (since he

already owns every Thomas the Tank Engine ever made) and he loves to travel.

Joshua has been famous throughout his life for his "passions." (Some would say "obsessions." But one man's "hobby" is another person's "obsession.") He's been through an elephant phase, shark phase, whale phase, warthog, peccary, rhino, and potbellied pig phase. He's always been passionate about steam locomotives, dinosaurs, and woolly mammoths. Some phases last a few months, some a few years. Now that you know this trait of Joshua's to latch onto a new interest, you'll understand why my brother responded to our trip destination by asking, "Is Josh into the Branch Davidians now?"*

When I posed the trip idea to Josh, he eagerly started to plan. He got on the internet, and soon told me that Waco, Texas is also the site of the largest concentration of mammoth fossils in North America. *And* that Waco has three—count them—THREE, Burger Kings! A zoo, mammoths, and Burger King? Waco—here we come!

He was quite enamored with taking pictures of each animal, cataloging each species for future artwork and info. He amazed our zookeeper friend by knowing the name of every animal they have at the zoo. He wasn't quite as thrilled with the slobber of a giraffe's tongue, the smell of rhino dung, or the screaming pitch of the screech monkeys. But he told me that this trip was "the best, most memorable days of my life." Quite a compliment from my teenager.

Joshua's life has been the source of many trips for my husband and me. It was Joshua who started us on our trip down the road of autism. When he was two and half years old, we took our first trip to a child psychiatrist, who told us that Joshua would never speak, that we should grieve over the loss of our child, and plan for him to be institutionalized. This trip initially got us lost, caught up on the freeway of autism and angst, full of potholes, and headed straight to despair. Thankfully, we stopped to check our directions, and were soon sent on a much smoother, albeit more complicated, trip down a much different road to hope and healing.

It was Joshua's needs that took us on a trip down the highway of therapies, with stops at auditory integration therapy, Applied Behavior Analysis therapy, sensory integration therapy, hippo therapy, music therapy, and many other destinations. We met terrific people on the way, and learned to avoid those stops that didn't appeal to us.

With Josh, we took trips to train museums in nine different states, saw zoos in every region of the country, visited Sea World, DisneyWorld, and a bison farm. Joshua has learned to pack his own suitcase and his backpack, full of everything he needs to have a good time. He has sometimes even tried to pack his light table, insisting that he needs it! We have had trips that were wonderful, like our trip to Hilton Head Island for a week of sun, surf, sand, and sea creatures. We have had trips that were miserable, like the trip to Ohio when we had to purchase a harness and leash to keep Zachary from running away from us. The boys have learned to handle airports, airplanes, flights without Coca-Cola, and towns without Burger King during these many trips, and we have learned that you truly can vacation with three boys with autism.

Josh showed us that the road we travel called autism can be funny, sweet, and highly entertaining at times. Josh is a junior in high school. He has paraprofessional support throughout his day at school, does well with academics, and has friends. He needs social instruction on a consistent basis to travel through the world of adolescence and high school. He laughs at jokes, goes to the movies by himself, reads vora-ciously, and volunteers three hours a week at the library. He still has autism; he sometimes flaps his hands, flicks his fingers in front of his eyes, and makes unusual sounds.

At 16, Josh has shown us, and everyone he has ever met, that autism is not a destination, but a journey. His final arrival point is still undetermined. He has made significant progress since his early, non-verbal, sensory-overwhelmed, screaming, miserable autism days. He didn't say anything inappropriate to anyone on our trip to Waco—not even to the Transportation Authority Agent who took his four ounce bottle of Liquid Paper away from him at the security checkpoint in the airport! I was actually disappointed—Josh's comments and perspec-tive are usually the source of much laughter for me! Because he was so "typical," I didn't have a really funny story to tell when we got home!

While I was traveling with him, I realized how far we both had come in the past 16 years. Josh was a peaceful companion—not asking for or needing a lot of conversation, and perfectly happy to watch Animal Planet on the hotel room TV and swim in the pool. I was quite bored most of the time, and managed to read four books over four days! He insisted on cruising through Target and Walmart, even though we have those stores in our own hometown.

Joshua goes to Burger King and Blockbuster every Friday. He rented "Hamlet" this past week (starring Kenneth Branagh) and has watched it non-stop. I have a feeling that he is about to take us on a trip through the works of Shakespeare—he's been walking through the house saying, "To be or not to be?" Rather profound, isn't it?

STRATEGIES FOR TERRIFIC TRAVEL

1. Use a Picture Schedule for Travel.

There are pictures available on the internet for literally everything and every location you can ever contemplate for a vacation. There are even pictures of the inside of airplanes, bus depots, and cabs in New York! Give your child a visual schedule of what to expect for each part of the trip. We use the maps of airports to help prepare them for the food selections we will have while we are waiting for a flight.

2. Find Out What Accommodations Your Destination Can Give to Your Family.

We took a week-long trip to Disneyworld, Florida, and had a wonderful time. We checked with their customer help desk before arrival, and the employee gave us terrific hints and supports on how to have a wonderful vacation with our boys. We had the same experience at SeaWorld, Busch Gardens, and numerous other amusement parks. The biggest help is not having to wait in line for rides or shows. If you ask for support ahead of time, then everyone is prepared.

3. Plan Well for the Airport, Flight, and Security Checkpoints.

We have frequently traveled on airplanes with the boys. In the process, we have learned to be open and honest about the boys and their autism. The following ideas helped make the airport experience positive.

a. Instead of getting on the airplane first, when the airline asks for people needing special assistance, we would get on absolutely last. My husband or I would discuss this with the gate agents, and explain that the worst part of flying is sitting on an airplane waiting for take-off. Craig would get on the airplane with our supplies and one child. I would keep the other two in the gate area until the attendant was making the final boarding call. Then we would join him on the plane, buckleup and takeoff.

b. I print labels with the international handicapped symbol on them, and we put the labels on our shirts and the boys' shirts (or backs, if they wouldn't leave the label alone!). This is a clearly visible cue to all personnel that the boys have a disability. Personnel always offer help without our even asking.

c. When we check in for the flight, we tell the desk agent that we have children with autism traveling with us, and security screening might be difficult. The agents can contact security, and they allow us to use the security line that is typically reserved for pilots and flight attendants. This shortens our wait time and the security personnel are more relaxed when we need to creatively get the boys through the screening process.

4. Take Breaks during the Vacation.

We found that the boys could not handle too much fun in one day! We frequently take breaks when traveling. This means we head back to our hotel or wherever we are staying, and don't do anything. At least, it looks like we aren't doing anything. But we are calming down, watching television or a movie, and escaping the "new" for time with the "familiar."

˙ The name "Branch Davidian" is most widely known for the Waco Siege of 1993 on their property (known as the Mount Carmel Center) near Waco, Texas, by the ATF, FBI, and Texas National Guard, which resulted in the deaths of their leader, David Koresh, as well as 82 other Branch Davidians and four ATF agents.

CHAPTER 26

You Might Be the Parent of an Autistic Child If . . . .

My husband, Craig, is a very funny man. I mean REALLY funny. His sense of humor is not only one of the things I love most about him, but also a trait that has kept me sane in the past 20 years of marriage. Recently, we were on a long drive together when I posed the question (as in Jeff Foxworthy's, "You might be a redneck if . . .") of what it means to be the parent of a child with autism. The following is our tongue-in-cheek-list for the statement, "You might be the parent of a child with autism if . . ."

- you can name *every* zoo or train museum within a six-state radius.
- you were the first one on the block to get the van with the DVD player, and you told your insurance company that it was therapeutic!

- you've put your child between two couch cushions, lain on top of her for 15 minutes, and called it therapy!
- you can open ketchup packets while driving.
- you have a swing INSIDE your house.
- you know there is a huge difference between Burger King fries and Wendy's fries.
- you know at least five of the following acronyms: MDC, IEP, SLP, OT, PT, ASA, DAN, CAN, GFCF, ABA, FT. (extra points if you know all of them!)
- your school district's superintendent greets you by your first name.
- you can name *all* of the Thomas the Tank engines—even the new ones!
- you have a strong opinion on who was the best Mr. Conductor: Alec Baldwin (no). George Carlin (yes). Ringo Starr (maybe).
- you do not know the meaning of the word *relax*.
- you can recite phrases from *all* the Disney films.
- you know the names of your state senator and representative, and you've written letters to them.
- your home does not have wallpaper or anything breakable in it, but it does have six locks on the doors.
- your idea of a family holiday dinner is chicken nuggets, Lucky Charms, and lemonade.
- you consider a "full night's sleep" to be four hours.
- you think ketchup counts as a food group.
- your child's wardrobe consists of, a) nothing with buttons; b) all one color; c) only sweat pants; d) all of the above.
- your child has run around naked in a public place.

- at your home, lunch is at 11:00 o'clock—NOT 11:03; 11:15; or 10:55, but at 11:00 o'clock!
- your pediatrician asks YOU, "What do you think we should do?"
- you break into a sweat if the phone rings while the kids are at school.
- you consider successful toilet training to be on a par with winning the lottery.
- all of your neighbors have you on speed dial.
- the last three books you read were by Tony Attwood.
- your bedtime is *after* the kids are at school.
- you think "R & R" is traveling to the next railroad museum.
- you send Christmas cards to more than two doctors or three teachers.
- your pharmacist has devised 30 different flavors for your child's prescription.
- you've replaced four toilets in a month because the toys were lodged too deep to repair them.
- you sometimes think that it would be easier to medicate yourself instead of your child.

AND MOST OF ALL,

- you know that the TRUE meaning of the word *joy* is housed within a glance, a sound, a word, a touch.

Strategies for Maintaining Your Sense of Humor

1. Autism Changes.

The challenges and characteristics of autism change over a lifetime. The child who screams when a dog barks at the age of two may want to own a dog at the age of 20. The person who is non-verbal at seven may be fluent with a communication device at 17. Realizing that your child will change, learn, and progress helps you keep a sense of humor and perspective during the challenging moments.

2. You're Not as Popular as You Think.

Truthfully, not everyone is watching you in the grocery store. Only one or two people. Wave at them. Smile at them. They'll be really uncomfortable, and you'll get to chuckle.

3. You Are Not Alone.

Sadly, there are more children with autism than ever in our world. Happily, that means that you are not the only parent who has ever had a child strip naked at the local park; nor are you the only one whose child eats Gummi Bears for breakfast. Get on Facebook or a blog or chat room and read some posts. You'll be laughing at the stories and the similarities in our lives. By the way, my current favorite is "The Autism Life" on Facebook. Reading a "Ewanism" every day keeps me laughing, even when my own children are not making me laugh.

CHAPTER 27

Step by Step:
Measuring Progress

For the past few months, I have been secretly thrilled with one of the signs of aging. I had no idea that my eyelashes would grow so much in my 40's! Every day, when I put on my mascara, I end up with little black dots on the top of my eyelids. I've never had long eyelashes that could almost touch my eyelids, and thought to myself, "Cool! I didn't realize eyelashes grew more as you got older."

Last week, the truth hit me while looking in the bathroom mirror. My eyelashes didn't grow! My *eyebrows* had *sagged*! What I thought was a tiny little perk of getting older is actually a huge indication that gravity is pulling everything I have toward my feet. My "glass-half-full" attitude had kept me from seeing the "gravity" of my situation (pun intended!).

The progress of time creeps up on all of us at some point. There is that day when the changes hit you square in the chest (yes, those too!) and remind you that everything is different. If someone had told me 15 years ago that I would be taking my Asperger's son to college 1,200 miles away from home, I would have either laughed hysterically or sobbed at their cruel jest. At four years of age, Spencer was barely speaking intelligible words, required every part of his day to be the same as the day before, and would cry hysterically if he was going somewhere new. The first week of a new school year was filled with anxiety, refusals, and tantrums over having to use a new book bag.

This week, my husband and I drove him to a college he has never seen (except online), to live in a state he's been to twice, in an apartment he's never seen, with roommates he's never met (and whose names he doesn't know) and with a class schedule that isn't finalized yet. And he's fine. I'm an anxiety-filled mess, but he's fine. He said to me, "Don't worry Mom. It'll be great."

Spencer and Joshua were diagnosed with autism in 1994 at the ages of three and two, and then Zachary in 1995 at the age of two. In 1995, we were privileged to be part of a research study being conducted by Dr. Catherine Lord at the University of Chicago. The boys' assessments were videotaped, which is standard practice in many places, and especially for research. My current work as part of a diagnostic team recently led me to attend training on using the Autism Diagnostic Observation Schedule (ADOS) which had been the assessment tool used in the boys' diagnosis. What I didn't realize in 1994 was that the boys were part of the research used to revise the ADOS assessment. At that time of our lives, we were barely coping on a daily basis, and the minor details, like what the research was really focused on, seemed to be beyond my grasp.

I contacted Dr. Catherine Lord after the training, and she graciously sent me copies of the boys' diagnostic videos. Not many of us get to see the clear, measured, and documented progress of our children. It was a humbling and amazing experience. To see the test being administered to each boy, and seeing their challenges and abilities within that context, was one of those moments when I felt the passage of time. It was a bittersweet experience; we saw the amazing progress of Spencer and Joshua, but also felt the distress of seeing Zach struggle with the same language and behavioral challenges at age three that he still struggles with today. I relived my exhaustion just watching the three of them on film. And was horrified at my hair style and clothing—what was I thinking?

I've also been transcribing anecdotes from the school communication notebooks that we used when the boys were in early childhood and elementary school programs. These notebooks went back and forth to school teams on a daily basis, with info about what they had said, skills achieved, and challenges analyzed. Transcribing these notes has also allowed me to see the progress they have made. To read my note to the teacher about how thrilled I was that Joshua followed my verbal direction to get in the car, or the excitement of Zachary sleeping five hours at one time reminds me that, although the boys still have significant struggles, there has been progress. Slow, then rapid, progression then regression—it's all documented amid the questions of meeting times, school functions, and forgetting to pack their lunch. Each anecdote of increased language or social understanding makes me smile and chuckle. I would have forgotten all but one or two of those instances if I hadn't written them down. Reading the stories makes me grateful Zach isn't still watching Bambi every day, happy that Josh sleeps until 9:00 a.m. on most days, and that Spencer no longer eats only white food.

The boys have *progressed*. No one told us that when they were young and we wondered what their lives would be like. Children with autism *progress*. This statement should be written on the bottom of every report, IEP or blog. They will not be the exact same person at 20 years of age that they are at two. Will they still have autism at 20? Probably. But it won't be the same "autism" that it was at the time of diagnosis. The progress may be astounding or it may be incremental. But there will be progress.

STRATEGIES FOR MEASURING PROGRESS

1. Keep an Organized Record of Documents.

Use any organizational system that makes sense for your situation. I used binders, one for each boy, with dividers by school year. Each section included final IEP with goal data, evaluations, copies of some academic work, artwork, and anything else that was important that year.

2. Keep a Journal.

This doesn't have to be anything fancy—a Word file on your computer, or a small notebook. Write the date, and what happened. Keep notes of anything funny, touching, exasperating, or sad. You may think that you will never forget what happened today—but you will!

3. Review and Re-evaluate.

At least once a year, review the progress of your child. I usually do this prior to an annual IEP. Review the IEP from the year before, and be ready to discuss the progress you've seen at the meeting.

CHAPTER 28

Frequently Asked Questions: A Guide for Self-Defense

I have the privilege of traveling to different parts of the country, sharing my tiny bit of insight into educating and raising kids with autism. I try to have time for a "Question and Answer" period following each presentation, because I enjoy the personal interactions with other families and professionals. I will get a variety of questions, but there are some asked frequently: Do the boys get along with each other? When did you realize your kids had autism? Have you tried the GF/CF diet? How do I get my school team to help with sensory integration? How do you handle the holidays? Does your extended family accept the diagnosis? Are there other members of your family with autism?

But the most frequently asked question is "How do you do it?" This question comes from a tearful mom of a newly diagnosed child, or a curious, interested teacher, or a school administrator. Each of them is wondering how I handle three kids with autism. Believe it or not, this is the hardest question that I'm asked. There are days when I don't think I "handle" it at all. In fact, you might be surprised to know that I actually question my parenting on a daily basis! I frequently think I'm the worst parent on the planet.

I'm not comfortable answering this question with some philosophical musing about how I know that my boys are gifts, or a critical dissertation on doing extensive reading and research. When asked how I cope, I usually respond with, "I drink a lot of Diet Coke." Although true, the serious or the funny answer doesn't get me through each day or each challenging moment. It's the practical things that help me handle the stress, stay cheerful during mood swings, and find some small joy on a daily, weekly, or monthly basis.

About once a month, I have my "D-Day." It stands for "Denial Day." I go into complete denial that I have children with autism. If they want to watch DVDs and eat Lucky Charms all day, that's fine with me. I am not their therapist, doctor, counselor, or a supermom. I'm just me. I sew, read a book, or drink Diet Coke all day, eat chocolate and basically become a sloth. But slothfulness for a day builds my energy for the rest of the month! I also play all day with my boys and leave the dishes until they're in bed.

One of my friends says that she believes my purpose in life is to make everyone else feel better about their own lives in comparison to mine. I think there are better ways of coping with challenges than thinking that someone else is more miserable! But if that's what you need, then I'm here for you.

STRATEGIES FOR RETAINING A SENSE OF SELF

1. Have a Hobby.

I'm serious. We all need something to fulfill our individual selves or we become martyrs to the cause. Find something that brings *you* joy—gardening, knitting, reading romance novels, scrapbooking, volunteering. It doesn't matter what it is—just that you make time to fulfill that need once a month. My son, Spencer, says that if I'm not with my children, he can always find me at the computer, my sewing machine, or my bed!

2. Teach Your Kids to Sleep.

Unfortunately, sleeping is a skill that will have to be taught to some of our kids with ASD. As difficult as it may be to teach, having kids who go to sleep for at least six hours a night is vital to your well-being. Sleep deprivation wreaks havoc on you physically, mentally, and emotionally—which is why it is a form a torture in times of war!

3. Use a Schedule.

Consistency and predictability are key issues for children on the spectrum. Following a visual/written routine for life at home will go a long way toward having a calm and enjoyable household. Using a schedule at home will also reinforce the using of schedules at school or work. Schedules assist in keeping me calm and enjoyable, too.

4. Choose One Challenge to Work on Each Month.

I can become overwhelmed at all that I need to do, teach, and work on with my guys. I try to work on only one goal a month for each of the boys. A very smart friend of mine says, "Pay your mortgage, your utility bills and choose a challenge on the 1ˢᵗ of every month." Being focused like this helps me to be successful in working on the challenge and keeps me a bit more sane.

5. Find a Support Group.

Support groups don't have to be official. A group of girl-friends, a women's group at church, a lunchtime gathering with coworkers—it doesn't matter how many people, just that you have a group who can consistently be there for you when you need to vent, or laugh, or cry. The crisis of today is the humor of tomorrow. But only if you have someone to share it with!

PART IV

Community Interactions

CHAPTER 29

"Do Neanderthals Hunt Mammoths Like We Pray?"

I t is difficult to write the experiences we have had with religion. Not because I'm uncomfortable with sharing the challenges and gifts that have come from participating in our faith, but because faith, religion, and belief in a higher being is such a personal decision. My family has chosen to practice our beliefs in a Christian religion. This chapter specifically addresses the challenges and issues of faith and religious worship. I am not attempting to promote my personal beliefs, nor to alienate those who believe differently than I do. But if you are looking for advice on autism and religious worship, read on. If not, skip to Chapter 30.

Raising three sons with autism has many different challenges. For many families, one of the most interesting challenges is attempting to attend church. A person with autism has a unique and often concrete, literal perception of the world, which can make it difficult to process the spiritual aspects of life. Trying to sit still while reading a book is difficult enough—sitting still and listening to a sermon? Nearly impossible.

When my boys were 13, 12, and 10 years of age, every weekend they asked the same question: "Is it a church Sunday?" They asked me this question for years in the frantic hope that they wouldn't be tortured for three hours that week. (Our church does a block of meetings for three hours on Sundays.) One of the biggest reasons they loved to go on vacation was because we wouldn't be attending church on Sunday!

This is not the typical whine of children who don't like sitting still or who would rather play outside. Our three sons have autism. Everything about the three hours of church is overwhelming and uncomfortable for them. There is just too much sitting, too many people, too much talking, and too much noise. Not to mention having to wear really uncomfortable clothing!

Beyond the environment issue, we have the greater challenge of children who think and learn differently than the rest of the world. Individuals with autism are concrete, literal thinkers. They are visual, kinesthetic learners. They have to see it, touch it, and experience it. For example: Every night, at 9:00 pm, we attempt to gather our boys together for prayer. My parents live with us, so they join in too. And our dog, Cody, who lies down in the middle of our circle. And, although they balk and protest at kneeling in the circle, our sons can do it.

One night, right after the "Amen," our 12-year-old son Joshua said, "Mom, do Neanderthals hunt mammoths like we pray?"

This would seem an odd question, but Joshua has autism. He thinks in pictures, and prehistoric animals and humans currently fascinate him. So I thought for a minute, and realized that with our family kneeling in a circle, and our dog in the center, we were in the same format as Neanderthals when they hunt mammoths—in a circle, with their prey in the middle!

Our children also struggle to understand another person's point of view, or to delve into inner thoughts and depths of emotion. So as the rest of us continually find new insight and understanding in the same scripture we read years ago, my boys just hear the same words over and over again. When Spencer was about eight, he was having a particularly difficult day in Sunday School and I was trying to calm him down in the hallway. Church members were walking up and down the hall. Spencer was quite agitated and yelled at me, "It's always the same! It's just 'Jesus this' and 'Jesus that!' Can we stop talking about Jesus?"

The response of other church members has been lovely and supportive. When the boys were young, and we were exhausted and stressed-out parents, church members would unexpectedly show up to stay with the boys so we could grocery shop without them. Church members volunteered to assist us in our home therapy program. Over the course of the past ten years, we have taught numerous classes about autism to classes of women, men, and youth at the request of our religious leaders. We have been unbelievably creative about how and when we attend church. We've had individual Sunday School teachers, classes taught at our home (instead of in the church building), visual systems put in place for the whole youth program, and practice sessions on how to participate in the passing of the sacrament.

Every time another church member finds out about our sons, I can guarantee that the next comment will be something along the lines of "The Lord must have loved you very much to give you these children." I think that the Lord could love me just a little bit less on some days! This is often the statement made by people who don't know what else to say to us. It's a bit like having a family member die—everyone wants to comfort you but doesn't know what to say. Others comment on how valiant and patient we are as their parents with the statement "I couldn't do what you have done." There have even been a few people who have honestly asked us why we work so hard to teach them because we know that "The Lord will forgive them everything."

I emphatically disagree with this "doctrine." I do not believe that my children chose to come to this Earth and be unable to tolerate other people, or communicate in ways others do not understand, or that they chose to struggle every day of their lives to understand the rest of the world. I do believe that my boys and I, and the rest of my extended family, chose to be together. I have had deeply spiritual confirmation of the eternal nature of our family. We are simply choosing faith in the Lord. We choose to follow the Savior, we choose to believe in His purpose and plan. No matter what that means on this Earth. Our faith says that we believe in the Lord, and the vagaries of this earthly life are part of His plan. I hope to someday have a conversation with Him about some aspects of "His plan," but for now, I am trying to seek His presence in our lives every day.

I believe that every family should be able to participate in the faith of their choice. My family and I will continue to encourage and teach our sons our beliefs as best we can, within the parameters of their learning ability. The boys have been baptized, will pass the Sacrament and perform sacred duties as they can. But their participation will never be exactly like everyone else's. When Joshua was getting ready for baptism, (which is done at the age of eight in our church) he was convinced that there were sharks in the water, so he refused to be baptized. His interview with our bishop was rather entertaining and he kept saying "But there are lemon sharks in the water!" Joshua struggles with sensory overload, so there are some days when the sound of the organ makes him want to hide under the pew. Zachary doesn't like the "quiet" silence of the Sacrament being passed, so he wears headphones. In the end, we have decided that we bring our children to church in the hope that they feel the spirit somehow. And that our sons will know another "community" of people who love and care about them. Our priority is not to teach scripture, doctrine, or obedience to tradition. But to teach the power of the Savior's love.

ZACH'S STORY

Our son Zachary has significant challenges with his autism. Since the onset of autism at the age of 16 months, he has struggled with language, aggression, sensory integration, and many other challenges too numerous to mention. Sitting still has never been his favorite activity, so attending church was very stressful for him. However, over the course of the past 16 years, we have worked to support him in our religious environment.

When Zach was three years old, and very anxious and frightened, my husband and I made the decision that Zach and I would not attend church at all. This was a very difficult decision for us, since we believe that attending church every Sunday is an important way to renew our covenants with the Lord. But Zach was unwilling to sit for more than three minutes, or even go into the building, so we felt that I could use those hours on Sunday in a more useful manner. My husband and our other two sons struggled through church, and Zach and I stayed home and worked on language.

When Zach was six, we felt that he was ready to tackle church. We met with our clergy and youth leaders and brainstormed with them some ideas we had for supporting Zach at church. They were amazingly supportive and we moved forward. We asked a woman in our congregation to be Zach's personal Sunday School teacher. She did not have a background in Special Education, but did have a background in teaching, and more importantly, the desire to serve Zach.

We began with having her come to our home to teach Zach. This was relatively easy in our situation, since we lived only five blocks from our church building. We had been utilizing a room in our home as a therapy room, and that's where she and Zach met. She and I had a meeting prior to their first Sunday; we set up a schedule, discussed activities, and a time frame. Initially, none of the activities they did were religious in nature—they were Zach's preferred and familiar activities like watching Thomas the Tank engine videos, doing sight words, color blocks, etc.

The first Sunday was traumatic for all of us. Zachary was not thrilled about dealing with a new person, I sat at the top of the stairs listening to him scream, and I think our teacher wondered what she had committed herself to! By the fourth or fifth Sunday though, Zach was much calmer, and so were we.

Our teacher was leaving one Sunday when she turned to me and said, "I've had inspiration about what I am to teach Zachary."

"Oh, really?" I said.

"Yes, I'm not supposed to teach him anything. I'm only supposed to love him." This simple statement moved me to tears, for it was exactly what we wanted for Zach.

After six months, we felt that Zach and his teacher were comfortable enough with each other and the routine for the next phase. We moved them both to the church building. We were able to have our own classroom, and they met for the first 30 minutes of Sunday School. This was a leap of faith for our congregation as well, since they could hear the sounds of the Thomas the Tank Engine video coming out of the Sunday School room!

Another six months and we began to work on Zach going in with the other kids. We accomplished this with small, steady steps, based on his interests and lots of rewards. For Zach, this meant music. Zach loves music, so his teacher had taught him to sing one of the simple youth songs with hand movements. We worked with the youth leaders, and spoke with the other children. Every Sunday, as soon as Zachary walked into the youth room, the other children and leaders stopped what they were doing (even in the middle of a scripture) and began to sing Zach's song! It was really funny—but it worked great! We then rewarded Zach with his favorite cookie for simply walking into the youth room.

We've had other children with autism in our congregation who have not needed this amount of support, but who still needed "breaks" during church, sensory input, and one-to-one assistance. Each child is different, but the basic principles still apply.

The result of all of this work went beyond just support for Zach. The whole congregation has learned to view "bad behavior" differently and to support all individuals with disabilities more patiently and compassionately.

The key to Zach's success was the communication we had with his teacher and the other youth leaders. Everyone was truly exhibiting Christ's love as they worked with us to support and love Zach. There were many "difficult" Sundays, but the feeling of community and commitment was strong for everyone.

As of today, Zachary sits through the whole Sacrament service with us, with minimal prompts and breaks. He is able to sit with the other children for almost 20 minutes, and then he and I go home. But it is enough time for both of us to feel the love of our fellow members and God's love.

STRATEGIES FOR FAMILY AND CLERGY

1. Be Realistic about Expectations.

If religious services are too long for the child, find an appropriate time to leave. When the boys were very young, we worked for months to stay for 20 minutes of the service—long enough for us to have the sacrament. When our youngest was learning to tolerate the youth services, we rewarded him for simply walking into the room with the other kids. Eventually, he stayed almost 25 minutes with the other children.

2. Provide a Visual Schedule of the Service.

There is a variety of clip art and other pictures that can be used to structure the activities for the child with autism. We used a file folder with Velcro and had pictures to indicate song, prayer, talking, scripture story, etc. The adults who ran our children's program had large copies of the pictures that were on the board in front of all the children. Each child who needed an individual schedule was provided a smaller version to follow.

3. Provide Alternate Activities for the Child.

Children with autism are easily overwhelmed by their senses. We provided a basket of sensory toys during the main service and during the youth service that children could use for calming themselves. We used headphones with music or books on tape for our boys to wear during the difficult moments. We also created a variety of activities (word matching, coloring, drawing, etc.) in file folders that were then put in a "Sunday Book" to use during the times it was difficult for them to pay attention auditorily.

4. Give Awareness Presentations.`

I highly recommend a presentation of some sort to the other members of the congregation that discusses the basics of autism, and what efforts are being made to support the children at church. Most people want to help, but don't know how. We had quite a few instances where members of our church would approach our boys during a meltdown and put their arms around the boys or hug them. This was the most natural, but worst possible, reaction! When we discussed this with others, they understood the appropriate way to support us during the difficult moments.

5. Visit the Church Building at Times Other than Sunday.

We often have other activities that take place at our church building, and it was difficult at first for the boys to make the mental shift in behavior. For example, sometimes a Halloween party is held at a church building. Children with autism think they are going to have to sit still—not have fun! And then the next Sunday, they want to run around the building again instead of sitting still! So we used a visual structure to show them what behavior would be expected during our visit to the building. Although this was initially stressful, eventually the boys learned that church was a place of fun and learning.

6. Practice Prayer and Scripture Time at Home.

It is easier to teach the proper behavior for prayer in short, calm moments at home.

CHAPTER 30

Shop 'Til You Drop:
The Woes of Walmart

My very first success in using a visual schedule with my boys occurred while shopping (which is absolutely appropriate given my penchant for retail therapy). When the boys were very young, and also very troubled by their autism, my husband frequently had to be out of town for work. So I was often alone with the guys, trying to figure out how to buy groceries, get gas for the car, and run the myriad of errands required to manage the household.

Spencer's first early childhood teacher was the catalyst for my "breakthrough" as a parent. She called one day to tell me how well Spencer was doing in school, and that he was doing a great job following a visual schedule. I asked her to describe a visual schedule for me. She proceeded to do so and then said, "This would be a great way to take him grocery shopping. He can follow a visual schedule indicating the items you need to purchase and then he will know when shopping will be finished."

You know the idiom, "A light bulb went off in my head"? That was exactly what happened at that moment. I quickly cut out pictures of food items that we needed from the newspaper; glued them onto a piece of paper in the order that we would buy them; and showed it to the boys. Then we got in the car and went grocery shopping. And, "Voila!" We actually managed to get everything we needed without someone screaming, running down the aisle, crying, or bolting out of the store!

Not all of our shopping expeditions have turned out well, however. I have left carts of groceries, or other items, sitting in the middle of an aisle while I carried a screaming, arch-backed child out of the store. I confess that I have also bribed them with the purchase of a box of cereal as a reward for staying with me in the grocery store. *Lucky Charms* was the reward of choice for my guys. They didn't actually eat the cereal; they just picked out the sugared marshmallows and threw the rest away. It felt like a waste of money until I realized that a $3.00 box of cereal allowed me to purchase my weekly groceries without the store manager or security having to be called!

Walmart has been the site of most of our struggles. I'm pretty certain that it's the environment that causes the stress overload—the aisles are narrow; the merchandise is piled high; the noise level is horrific and the sheer quantity of "stuff" is visually overwhelming. Last Christmas, while shopping in Walmart, Joshua began to get irritable, loud, and rude. When I asked him what was wrong, he said, "TOO MUCH MERCHANDISE. I WANT TO GO TO TARGET!" (I'm fairly certain we won't ever be the spokespeople for Walmart!)

I've found that it's while we're out in our community shopping that we also get the most comments from onlookers. I'm always baffled by the attitude of some people who believe that I really want their input on my parenting skills. I get a lot of "he just needs some discipline" or "if you would spank him every once in a while he wouldn't act like that." I used to not respond, feeling ashamed and embarrassed at my inadequacy as a parent. Then, somewhere along the line, I decided that I really wanted to respond. So now, I typically respond with, "Zachary (or one of the other boy's names) has autism, and both he *and I* are doing the very best we can." This usually stuns people into silence, or, more frequently these days, I get a response of, "Oh, I should have known. My next door neighbor has autism."

It was on one of these shopping nightmares that I truly embraced the power that responding can have on unwanted criticism. We were in Walmart (where else?) in the checkout lane. Zach wanted a bag of skittles, and I was calmly telling him *no*. He was yelling, pacing, and getting ready to move into a major struggle. The older lady in line behind me made a comment about my inability to control my child. I gave her my response (see above) and turned away to work with Zach. The cashier leaned over to the elderly woman and said, "You ought to be ashamed!" I was stunned! Then the cashier said to me, "What can I do to help?" I looked at her for a moment, and told her that if someone could push my cart, I would carry Zach out of the store and to the car. She turned off the light at her check-out lane, grabbed my cart herself, and started walking out the door with me! On the way to my car she said, "Serves her right for being so rude to you!"

Joshua and Zachary had a habit of throwing themselves to the ground when they were really unhappy. We called it the "Superman" pose—face down on the floor, arms stretched out in front of them, legs splayed in back. When it gets to this point, there is nothing I can do except wait for their emotions to stabilize. This is not the time for me to use visuals or intervene in any way, as they have lost control. I typically stand near them, operating much like a yellow floor sign to warn others that there is a wet floor nearby. Eventually, the boys will calm down and get up and follow directions. One day (again in Walmart) Zach had a challenging moment, and threw himself to the ground in the middle of a main aisle. I took my position as "guard" and calmly waited him out. A young girl and her mom were walking toward us, and I heard the girl ask her mom, "What's wrong with him?" At this point, they were close enough to me that I answered, "He's just having a bad day." The mom woefully shook her head and said, "I'm going to join him!"

Clearly, for parents of children with autism, the sentence, "Shop 'til you drop," has a whole different meaning!

STRATEGIES FOR SUCCESSFUL SHOPPING

1. Have a Plan.

The words "window shopping" do not exist in the vocabulary of a person with autism. If you are in a store, you should be buying something. This means that all shopping expeditions need to be planned for purpose, length of time, and specific needs. Thankfully, having a grocery list is not only helpful for the person with autism, but the financial experts tell us that we will spend less money if we have a list!

2. Use a Visual System.

Create a visual system with a series of pictures for the items you will be purchasing. The pictures don't have to be item-specific; the pictures could be categories of food, dry goods, shoes, clothing, etc. As you go through the store, show the visual system to the person with autism and indicate how much more needs to be purchased before leaving. A reward, visualized with a picture at the end of this schedule, will be very helpful for the person who does not like to be in stores.

3. Be Prepared to Leave.

If the person with autism has a challenging or crisis moment while at the store, drop everything and leave. If you call the store after you leave, and explain where you left your grocery cart or items, and why you left, they will frequently hold the items for you until you can get back to the store.

4. You Can't Always Get What You Want.

Most of the time, the real struggle with shopping is that the person with autism insists on purchasing an item every time they are in the store. Whether it's food, a toy, a movie or some other item, the person has created a routine that must have a purchase in it. This is NOT lifelong behavior that you or anyone else wants. Start by creating a visual system of purchases to be made that includes the preferred item. Use the system, pointing out each item purchased, for the first few times you shop in the store. Then plan for a very short trip into the store that includes only one or two items. On this trip, put a "Change" card on the schedule, and picture *only* the item you will purchase. Put the picture of the item they want at the end of the schedule, to be received *after* they are home. This will allow you to reward the person with the preferred item after he or she has successfully walked through a purchase routine without the item included. For some individuals, you may need to give the reward immediately after the purchase is made. Others may need to get the preferred item once they are in the car. The key is to move the presence of the preferred item further and further away from the purchase routine. Eventually, show the person a visual schedule that doesn't include the preferred item at all. When they are able to consistently complete a store purchase routine without a behavior challenge, then you can create a schedule that allows them to randomly achieve the preferred item.

5. When All Else Fails . . .

If a trip to the store is currently just not within your energy level or the person's capabilities, then check into your local store options. Grocery stores will frequently accept a faxed grocery list, pull all the items for you, and you just have to walk in, pay for it, and leave. Many stores offer online shopping. If the delivery fee is too high, then ask a neighbor or friend to pick it up for you.

CHAPTER 31

Full Disclosure:
What to Say and When

I spend a good portion of my professional life diagnosing individuals with autism. Through hours of testing, observation, and interaction, a diagnosis is given via report and conference with the family. Although the diagnosis is written in the last pages of the report, it is the first item I discuss in the family conference. I have found that the discussion of how the diagnostic team arrived at the diagnosis and the recommendations is understood better if the diagnosis is already in the vocabulary.

This process has also been true for telling others about the boys' diagnosis. I have found that telling others about the diagnosis of autism is better than letting a situation fall apart and *then* sharing the information with the people involved. Spencer had a much more positive experience in the first few Cub Scout meetings when I told the adult leaders that he had autism, as opposed to his experience in Karate class when I decided not to tell the teacher about his autism but "wait and see what happens" and THEN tell the teacher if we needed to. People in the community are more patient and tolerant if they know *before* the child struggles, that this child might have difficulty with auditory instructions.

I am frequently asked by parents when to tell others (extended family, sport coaches, neighbors, friends' parents) about their child's autism. The question is almost always accompanied by the statement, "I don't want him/her to be labeled." So here is the hard truth: Your child is ALREADY labeled.

If the diagnosis of autism is appropriate, your child or adolescent has some odd or unusual ways of behaving, speaking, and interacting. Everyone involved in their life, whether significantly or fleetingly, KNOWS that they are different. So which label would you rather your child have—freaky, rude, obnoxious, stupid, weird? Or different, interesting, funny, autistic?

Each of us has a "label." I am labeled: female, Midwesterner, quilter, gardener, mother, best friend, Type A, Polly-Anna, and forgetful-of-details!

Each of these "labels" gives you insight into who I am, and an opportunity to speak with me and connect with me. The labels are a path to connectedness and understanding.

This is also true for the label "autism." It is a word that provides a path to connectedness and understanding for others. It does not define the person, just as "quilter" doesn't define me. And fellow quilters who meet me, still don't know exactly what type of quilter I am, or my favorite quilt block, or whether I quilt by hand or machine. There is still more to know about me. Knowing a person has autism allows others to begin a conversation or interaction with some perspective. And provides an opportunity to learn more about them.

Talking to the Person

We told Spencer and Joshua about their autism when they were eight and seven years old, respectively. This translated to 3rd grade and 2nd grade in our school system. We chose this time frame because they were beginning to notice that our family was a bit different than others, and because other students were also differentiating between their behavior and our boys' behavior.

We started the discussion by looking at pictures of random families that I had pulled off the internet. I printed pictures of families that looked alike or were wearing the same color shirt, etc. We asked the boys to tell us what they noticed about the families. They mentioned how similar each family member was to each other. We discussed the concept that some families all wear glasses, some families all have red hair, some families are tall—and our family has autism. The boys were very aware of Zach's struggles and we then explained that each of them had some autism, but that it was different than their brother's. That seemed like enough of an explanation for them at that point.

A few years later, I purchased the book, *Asperger's: What Does It Mean to Me?* by Catherine Faherty. This is a workbook that guides discussion through different aspects of autism and Asperger's. The interactive nature of the information was a wonderful way for me to individually discuss each boy's autism with him. We completed pages of the book based upon what autism characteristic was the strongest in their lives then. The boys were so excited about making their own book about their thoughts, feelings, and lives that they frequently took the book to school to share with their teachers and friends. Through the worksheets, I found out things I had never known. I found out that Spencer was struggling to hear the teacher because he sat by a window and could hear the cars pull up in front of the school each day and was overwhelmed by the sound. I found that Joshua felt like "syrup" when he ate ice cream. Each section of the workbook allowed us to explore and discuss not only how they processed the world around them, but also to teach them how others processed the world.

Telling our sons about their autism allowed us to give context to situations that they didn't understand. For instance, when a particular Boy Scout meeting had been problematic for Spencer, I was able to revisit the situation later and share that the other Scouts had been happy about going camping that weekend instead of later in the month, but that his autism made him not like things to change, so he was not happy. I explained to him that the other Scouts were cheering because they were happy at the change, and that he was yelling and angry because of his autism.

I believe that knowing personal strengths and challenges is empowering. Unless each of us knows where we struggle, we don't know when to ask for help. Knowing our strengths and skills allows us to share those talents with others. Individuals with autism know that they are different than other people—even those without verbal skills. Giving them the context of understanding why they feel so different allows them to accept and embrace their difference.

I want to be clear about this issue of telling a person that he or she has autism. Autism is the *reason* for certain behaviors—not an excuse. For a period of time, Joshua would justify his yelling, or inappropriate comments with the statement, "But it's my autism! I can't help it!" I completely understand why he may burst out with a literal statement about someone's weight, but the statement is still not socially appropriate. Acknowledging someone's autism should not give them permission to behave inappropriately or negatively. Likewise, having a child with autism does not give *us* permission to behave inappropriately or negatively toward others—no matter what comment is made about your child!

Talking to Classmates

Every school year, I did a presentation to the boys' classmates about autism and how it related to their classmate. I didn't use the exact word, "autism," until the students were in third grade—up until that point, I would discuss differences in people, and be more general in our conversation. These presentations typically occurred within the second week of school. The school team and I would choose a time frame that allowed the boys' classmates a few days to adjust to school again, and spend enough time with each other that they had some knowledge of what made their classmate different.

These classroom presentations for my boys have provided some of the most thought-provoking, touching, hilarious experiences in my life. I never tire of talking to other students about their classmate with autism! I've also done numerous classroom presentations for other students with autism, and the experience is always a highlight of my day. Here are a few of the most interesting presentation experiences:

- I asked Joshua's first grade classmates if they had noticed anything different about Joshua. A student raised her hand and said, "He can read and we can't!"

- I asked Spencer's fourth grade classmates what made Spencer seem different to them. A student told me that "Spencer can hear footsteps coming down the hall and know whether it is our teacher or the principal so he warns us if we are being too noisy. No one else can tell whose footsteps are coming."

- Joshua's second grade classmates told me that they thought he was "from the future" because he thought like a computer and was very smart.

- In Spencer's third grade class, I asked the students if they had ever heard the word "autism." A student raised his hand and told me that his dad had read in magazine that there was a guy in a hospital in Oklahoma who could cure autism but no one would let him out of the hospital. I have no idea where this information came from but it made me laugh!

When Zachary began Kindergarten, he was still struggling to use verbal language and manage physical aggression. I did my presentation to his fellow Kindergartners on the seventh day of school. At the end of the school year, Zach's school team and I decided to have someone interview the class about their experience with Zach. We were trying to decide if Zach should fulfill his IEP goals in a regular education classroom or in a smaller setting. I asked a friend to come interview Zach's classmates so that they would be honest and open about the experience. She initially just chatted with the class about what they had liked about Kindergarten, what was hard, etc. Then she asked them if any of their classmates ever did something that made them nervous? She didn't want to dictate what they would say, so she didn't use Zachary's name at first. This question of being nervous around another student was met with silence, and puzzled looks. She elaborated by saying, "You know, sometimes kids will do things that we don't understand or make us scared. Has that ever happened?" A little girl raised her hand and said, "Do you mean like when Zachary's screams really loud?" My friend replied, "Yes, like that!" Another young boy popped up and said, "Well, that just makes the teachers unhappy!"

In the presentation I do with middle school students, I have them "experience" autism from a sensory overload perspective. I always ask for a volunteer from the class to be the person to get the sensory overload. The experience lasts 30 seconds. At the end of it, one young man walked to his desk and vomited! I was horrified that I had caused him to be ill, but the other students looked just as horrified—because they thought that each person with autism felt like vomiting every day! One of the students piped up and said, "I'm never going to be mean to Adam again!" ("Adam" was the student with autism in their class.)

*For a sample classroom presentation that you can use with your own child, please see the Appendix.

Talking to Strangers

For me, the most difficult decision of disclosure is when I'm standing in the middle of a store with a screaming, unhappy child and everyone around me is staring at us. Those are the moments that I wish I had the word "autism" tattooed across my forehead so that I didn't have to explain anything.

The early years of autism were the hardest for our family. My husband frequently was out of town, and I needed to handle the chores of raising children and running a household. This meant that

I was often alone in the grocery store/bank/hardware store, etc., with three boys under the age of five, all of whom had autism. I've left more grocery carts full of food and supplies standing inside a store than you can imagine because I had to take a screaming child OUT of the store. It's amazing to me how many people feel the need to comment on my parenting skills while I'm trying to comfort or assist a miserable child. The negative comments from strangers about me and my children used to make me angry or sad or defeated. I finally realized that most people are ignorant—they have no idea that my child is different and needs different parenting. And it was up to me to "educate" instead of "annihilate."

I decided that I would respond with the common courtesy that the people judging me appeared to lack. So if Joshua was stimming very loudly and a person told me to "get control of my child" I would say, "Joshua has autism. The noise in here makes him jumpy." If Spencer made an inappropriate comment to someone about their greasy hair, I would say, "Spencer has autism and he is learning to not say what he thinks. He'd like to apologize" and then make Spencer apologize.

Responding to strangers in the community, and disclosing the presence of autism, is empowering and powerful. More often than not, after I disclose the issue, people will tell me they have a nephew with autism, or they have a neighbor with autism. Or they are shamed into silence! Either response is fine with me. I feel better for teaching them that autism lives in their community and for advocating for my family.

CHAPTER 32

Autism Olympics: The Hundred-Yard Parking Lot Dash

I am not the greatest athlete, but I am a complete Olympic Games junkie. The Summer Games of 2008 provided endless hours of entertainment for me. I feel so connected to others from around the world by watching their triumphs and struggles to push themselves to physical limits when most of us won't even attempt to climb two flights of stairs!

I imagine we would feel more connected to other parents with autism if our every stunning feat was broadcast for others to see. Would we be motivated to teach our child to independently brush his or her teeth, if we saw other parents succeed in that endeavor? If we could see the numbers of families with autism parade into an arena for the Autism Olympics Opening Ceremony, would we feel the same sense of pride and exhilaration that we do watching the athletes enter?

We are Autism Athletes—every one of us. I think that raising a child with autism is just like being an Olympic athlete. Really, there is no difference between a gymnast doing a floor exercise and trying to get a screaming child off the floor of the grocery store. A swim medley of breaststroke, backstroke, freestyle, and butterfly, if done out of water, would look a lot like a five-minute self-stim episode. We've competed in the high jump and pole vault each time we've run after a child, jumping fences, foliage, and toys to keep them from running into the street. Our Decathalon is called a "De-caf-alon" every time we try to get through a day without caffeine. We are gold medalists in wrestling, attempting to keep clothes on a child who is determined to be naked.

There are obscure Olympic events like curling, kayaking, or shooting. We have obscure autism events like string spinning, random hand waving, and interpretive echolalia. My youngest son would win the gold medal in the interpretive echolalia event!

Watching Usain Bolt, the fastest man on Earth, racing in the 2008 Summer Olympics was the most amazing thing. But he can't hold a candle to a child in Toys "R" Us in search of the latest Thomas the Tank Engine!

In the opening ceremonies, some small countries have one to five athletes; larger countries have hundreds. But all the athletes who are able, come to the opening ceremony. If we were to hold an autism opening ceremony, it would truly show the world the number of people affected—even in small countries—and I bet we would fill the stadium in Beijing and beyond!

Like Olympic athletes, our ability to sustain high degrees of diffi-culty diminishes with age—sometimes our children improve and can no longer compete to be the best in autism. Our goal for competition is the exact opposite of Olympic athletes—we will try to lose the games of the Autism Olympics and work really hard to disqualify ourselves from competition. Yet many of us will compete for years, maybe the rest of our lives. And win a gold medal every time!

Although my husband and I are not athletically inclined, we still wanted our sons to participate on a sports team. At least, that's what we wanted before they were born. After the autism diagnosis, we rethought our visions of Olympic glory.

Spencer was very coordinated as a young child. He could dribble a basketball at 18 months of age. He could hit a baseball with a bat every time we threw it at him. He could throw a football directly to us. Maybe he could bring us fame, glory, and early retirement by playing a sport.

We registered him for Little League baseball at the age of eight. Other kids had started playing at age four, but we felt that his ability to always hit the ball would make up for the years he spent playing in therapy instead of on the baseball diamond. The Little League team needed a coach, so I volunteered. I know what you're thinking—but I traveled with the high school baseball team keeping their statistics. I can still tell a curve ball from a slider, and calculate Earned Run Average.

I coached the team and kept Spencer focused on the game. Craig would pace the sidelines during the games, worried that Spencer wouldn't be able to hit the ball when it really mattered. But he did. He hit the ball every time. And he yelled and ranted at his teammates when they missed hitting the ball. He couldn't understand why they would miss. Baseball was not going to be our ticket to fame.

We thought about other sports. Basketball? When we tried it, Spencer hit every child who got too close to him. Soccer? He said it was confusing because it looked like the other players were "ants on an anthill" running around the field.

He needed a sport that allowed him to be part of a team, but relied only on his individual skills for success. Martial arts was a turning point for Spencer. He was successful and part of a group. The visual aspect of watching the sensei perform the routines appealed to his learning style. The quiet atmosphere appealed to his environmental needs. And the ability to earn different colored belts as he progressed appealed to his ego!

Joshua has never wanted to participate in a sport. His idea of exercise is going to the mailbox each day. Zachary used up so much energy bouncing and pacing each day he didn't need a sport. Eventually, we had Zach walk the bridge over the Mississippi river in our town every few days to add more exercise.

We still aren't a "sport-oriented" family. Except when the Olympics are on!

STRATEGIES FOR INCLUDING SPORTS AND EXERCISE

1. Evaluate the Sport Requirements against the Person's Skills.

Every sport requires a certain skill set. Listing the person's abilities alongside the sport requirements can help determine what sport, if any, would be motivating. If the child finds heavy, weight-bearing sensory activities enjoyable, then bowling—or weight-lifting—could be a great sport. If the person is fascinated by numbers and calculations, then maybe being a manager or statistician for a school team would be a better fit than actually playing the sport.

2. Ask the Coaches or Team Organizers for Help.

Talk to the adults involved prior to starting participation and outline your child's strengths and where you think there will be challenges. Offer to help. Bring the equipment, organize the transportation, or coordinate the schedule. But be willing to help the coaches succeed as much as you want them to help your child succeed.

3. Investigate Special Olympics.

Special Olympics has wonderful and amazing programs. Find the program nearest you and speak with the organizers about available sports and practices.

4. Exercise is a Lifelong Skill.

If organized sports is not possible, find a way to teach daily exercise. Forty-five minutes of cardio, calorie-burning exercise is important for everyone. There have been some studies indicating that daily exercise of this nature can significantly decrease challenging, aggressive behavior.

Some individuals with autism do not enjoy exercise. Use their special interests to encourage physical activity. One young man I worked with really enjoyed puzzles. We put the puzzle board at one end of a hallway, and the puzzle pieces at the other end. In order to complete the puzzle, he had to walk back and forth in the hallway. Eventually, the distance was increased until he was walking over five miles a day.

CHAPTER 33

An Apple a Day:
Healthcare Interactions

T he first time I mentioned to our new family physician that I was
concerned about Joshua's development, he didn't tell me I was
being neurotic. He listened with patience to my description and questions
about Joshua's random responses to his name, unusual behaviors while
watching television, and his consistently miserable demeanor. This was
the first time we had met this physician, because we were new to the
community. But he didn't dismiss my concerns. He sent Josh and me for
a developmental evaluation.

When I called our physician after the evaluation and told him that
the team felt that Joshua was showing the signs of autism, he asked me
to come to his office and meet with him. I thought this was an odd
request, but made the appointment. At our meeting, he listened to me

explain what the evaluation team had said, and responded, "Alyson, your description of Joshua and my observation of him led me to the same diagnosis. I know this because I have a son with autism."

This connection with our family physician made accepting the diagnosis somewhat easier. The next two medical professionals we saw were not as understanding and treated Josh and our family as research subjects without emotions or feelings. Over the course of our lives, we have had both positive and negative interactions with the medical profession. I won't spend time on the negative experiences—the only value in sharing the emotional misery of those interactions comes through what we learned.

Eventually, our boys were officially diagnosed at the University of Chicago by Dr. Catherine Lord and team. Dr. Catherine Lord is the clinical and creative mind behind the Autism Diagnostic Observation Scale (ADOS) which is used to diagnose autism or autism spectrum disorders in children and adults. This standardized test is used around the world by researchers and physicians. We were lucky to be living in the Chicago suburbs when Dr. Lord was revising the ADOS and took our three boys to be evaluated by her team. We had a very positive experience. The boys have been through other diagnostic assessments throughout their lives; sometimes as a component of a research study, sometimes to assess progress, and sometimes to provide updated information when applying for services.

Children with autism are still children, with all the attendant childhood problems and illnesses. The challenge comes when the child with autism does not like strangers touching them, or the feel of having their clothes off! A "well-child" visit with one of our boys often ended with everyone—including the physician—frustrated, crying, and wanting to run away.

All three boys got chicken pox the same summer. All three boys had chicken pox everywhere on their bodies—between their fingers, their toes, in their ears, on the bottoms of their feet, and on their private parts. And all three boys HATE to have lotion on their skin! They wouldn't get into the bath tub when I put the calming oatmeal powder into the water. They would scratch the chicken pox and cause the blisters to spread and bleed, which was another problem, because they wouldn't allow Band-Aids on their skin. I was getting to the end of my patience so I called our pediatrician for help.

Our pediatrician went through the basic list of remedies and listened to my reasons why each one of the remedies would not work with my boys. She was quiet for a moment, and said, "Well, let me send a note out to my fellow physicians and I'll get back to you." Later that day, she called and with laughter in her voice said, "My friend who is a veterinarian has an idea for you. Use one of the outdoor liquid fertilizer spreaders attached to your garden hose. Instead of filling the container with fertilizer, fill it with the oatmeal powder or anaesthetizing lotion and some water. Let the boys play outside with the hose and get themselves soaked with the soothing water." Brilliant!

Most of our interactions with the medical profession have occurred because of the need for dental work to be done in the hospital under anesthesia. Our first experience with a hospital was with Joshua having four root canals and two teeth removed. He was edgy, nervous, and frantically stimming when we arrived. His hand-flapping, bouncing, and vocalizing caused quite a few wide-eyed looks from the nurses but they gamely directed us to our room in same-day surgery. Josh was getting more nervous every time a nurse entered the room to ask us another question, or instruct him to take his clothes off. He was quickly becoming hysterical, which we knew would lead to hitting, kicking, and biting. One of the nurses said, "I have an idea," and left the room. She returned with a Polaroid camera and asked Josh if she could take his picture. He stopped mid-stim and said, "Sure!" then posed as if he was on the runway in a tuxedo and not in a hospital room with a tied-on gown flashing his naked bum! The nurse then offered to let him take pictures of everyone else. That simple activity calmed him down, and allowed us to get him ready for his surgery.

Zachary has also had dental work done under anesthesia numerous times. At the age of eight, Zach had not yet had his teeth cleaned, so our dentist felt that we needed to put him under anesthesia to thoroughly check his teeth and clean them. When we arrived at the hospital, the same-day surgery area did not have separate rooms, but curtains dividing beds in a large area. Zachary was frightened, which meant that he was screaming and desperately trying to flee. I was holding him as tightly as I could and began to sing. Zachary was calmed by singing at this age, so I started through my repertoire of Veggie Tales and Disney songs. As he began to calm, the anesthesiologist approached us. She held out a small cup with a pill in it toward me, and I shook my head "no" while still singing. She left, and came back with a syringe; then she held it out to me with a questioning face. I nodded "yes" and kept singing. One of the nurses said to the anesthesiologist, "maybe you need to sing too." The anesthesiologist looked panicked and said, "But I don't know the song!"

I sang the words, "I'll hold him while you give him the shot," and prepared to hold tight when Zach felt the pinch of a needle. We got through the shot of preliminary anesthesia, and Zach began to nod off. As I gently laid him on the waiting gurney softly, starting to stop my singing, he bolted upright and threw himself off the table. I grabbed him and began singing again. The nurses said, "Keep singing mom!" After another five minutes, I tried to lay him down again and cease singing. Nope. He bolted up and tried to flee. As I laid him down again, singing "When You Wish Upon a Star" the anesthesiologist said, "Keep singing and walk with us." I then had the most surreal experience as I walked through the operating rooms, through surgically garbed medical professionals, singing "When you wish upon a star, makes no difference who you are...." As we entered his assigned surgical room, his gloved and gowned dentist looked up, startled by the sight of his patient on a gurney accompanied by a singing parent!

Zachary's second trip to the hospital for dental work occurred five years later. We received a call from the surgical department telling us to be at the hospital at 6:00 a.m. because surgery was scheduled for 10:00 a.m. I explained Zachary's autism, and asked if there was any way we could be called just prior to his actual surgery time because waiting in the surgery suite for four hours would not go well for anyone. After phone calls between physicians, our dentist called to say that she would call us just before she was done with the patient ahead of Zach and we could head to the hospital then. The whole medical team was very accommodating and supportive of our concerns and Zach's needs. Which became rather challenging when Zach realized that we were going to a hospital!

Craig and I had to carry him into the same-day surgery room, kicking, screaming, and scratching us. We closed the door behind us—right on the nurse's face! From then on, Craig or I would stick our head out the door and tell the nurses what we needed. They handed us Band-Aids, told us to weigh him, and eventually gave us the medicine that would help him relax. By the time he was in surgery, all three of us were bleeding somewhere on our body. After the dental work was done, our dentist came into the room with us and said, "He has great teeth!" I thought to myself, well great. Now I can say, "our Zach is non-verbal, angry, and aggressive—but he has great teeth!"

Strategies for Managing Health Care

Visits to the Doctor

1. *Make an Appointment with the Doctor for the First Appointment in the Morning or the Last Appointment of the Day.*

Taking these appointment times will reduce the waiting time.

2. *Ask to Stay in the Waiting Room until the Doctor is Ready to Walk into the Exam Room.*

Most nurses will accommodate this need if you explain what happens if you wait too long in an exam room!

3. *Take Someone with You to Doctors' Appointments.*

Whether it's a check-up or an evaluation, having another adult with you is incredibly helpful. After the physician does the needed exam, you can send your child with the other adult to go get a treat, or go to the car while you ask the physician questions. Trying to discuss concerns with a physician and keep your child from having a meltdown at the same time is impossible!

4. Keep a Medical Record.

List dates, medications, dosages prescribed, responses, evaluations, illnesses—everything! It's amazing how much you forget when the physician is firing questions at you. Having the information written and available is very helpful.

Visits to the Hospital

1. Ask Questions and Share Information.

Nurses are the professionals who make everything happen in hospitals. They are the ones who can ensure a positive experience for you and your child—so tell them what your child needs, and ask for their help.

2. Discuss the Recovery Room.

Although it is standard procedure for the family members to be called after the patient is out of the recovery room, this procedure can cause trauma to the person with autism. We knew that when Zach woke up groggy from anesthesia and found his arms taped with IV (intravenous) lines, he would freak out and probably yank out the IV's and cause more problems. So we spoke with the surgical team and agreed that we would be with him immediately following surgery. We also asked that his IV be removed as soon as possible, which usually meant that it was removed before he was fully awake.

3. Use Visuals.

A visual schedule of what will happen is critical to helping the person stay calm. Especially when they are groggy from surgery. A picture indicating a favored activity or drink that they can have after they get home from the hospital will be clearer than the verbal assurance.

There are visual schedules available that show the process of getting an x-ray, blood draw, and a variety of other basic medical procedures. These schedules are very helpful and can be purchased or created.

Visits to the Dentist

1. Practice, Practice, Practice.

To say that our boys did not like the dentist is a massive understatement. We worked out a practice schedule with our dentist to allow the boys to slowly adjust to the process of having their teeth cleaned. Initially, we would walk into the office, say hello to the receptionist, and leave. Then we would sit on a chair and leave. Sit on the chair, look at the implements, and leave. Sit on the chair, brush our teeth, and leave. We would slowly add more steps of the teeth cleaning process into our visits until they were able to have a complete check-up.

2. Be Aware of Sensory Processing Difficulties.

Joshua and Zachary struggled to relax while having their teeth cleaned. I found that covering them with the weighted lead apron used during x-rays really helped them relax.

EPILOGUE:

The Real Mom

Like most parents, I am required to be the family policeman. I am judge and jury over disputes. I mete out sentences as necessary. I make rules, and I teach rules. Obviously, I am not always the most well-like person in my household!

I vividly remember the day when Spencer got mad enough to threaten me with getting a "different Mom." Perversely, I was thrilled with his statement! He understood my emotional need to belong to him! He responded verbally to his anger! He realized that another mom might actually let him eat waffles every meal for the rest of his life! Woo-hoo!

We actually taught the boys to argue. Okay—I know this sounds twisted. But arguing and refusing (appropriately) is a lifelong skill that we all need. Think about it—in order to argue, you have to understand

and acknowledge another's point of view, recognize your own opinion, and demand a response. It's a two-way conversation. And you should be able to do it without hitting someone! So we worked on teaching the boys how to verbally tell each other, "Give me back my toy," or "No, I want it," etc., with our prompting them in the background.

We found out later that our teaching left much to be desired. One day, while in the car, I heard Josh repetitively singing "Row, row, row your boat, row, row, row your boat, row, row, row your boat...." Spencer was responding with "Josh, please stop that." There's a pause, but the singing continued. "Joshie, please stop, I don't like that singing!" There's another pause, then the singing escalates in pace and volume. Spencer says, "JOSH!" Then Josh replies, "Okay, Okay. Now it's your turn—you sing and I'll be the mad person!"

As they've gotten older, the boys have gotten really good at protesting and telling me they are not happy with me. This is a sample of my all-time favorite responses:

- "You're fired!" (Wow, this sounds good to me!)
- "You do that again, Mom, and I'm taking away your lipstick!" (Oh no! Not my lipstick!)
- "You two-faced son of a jackal!" (What is a jackal? And do I look that bad today?)
- "You are being an angry buffalo!" (Hmmm . . . would I rather be a jackal?")
- "I will not bow to you!" (Oh yes, you will!)

Most of the time, these wild statements of misery roll off my back. I am brutally consistent and calm. I have learned, through years of experience, not to laugh, cry, or yell back. I repeat the instruction given and/or the consequence calmly and firmly. We've also used a variety of behavior techniques taught to us by experts in the field. And then there are some days when they threaten to "call the police" and I think a quiet cell and three meals a day sounds just fine with me.

A few years ago, the boys and I were driving home from speech therapy, and Joshua wanted to go to Burger King. His request was denied, which caused him to be furious with me. At this time, he was passionate about SpongeBob SquarePants, and watched the episodes constantly. So when I refused to detour for fast food, the following conversation ensued, which is a "personalized" modification of a SpongeBob episode:

"That's it! Five Questions to see if you're the REAL mom. Question number one, what time does Burger King open?"

Since you know of his addiction to Burger King, you understand why this is a very important question. I reply, "Well, that would be 7:00 a.m."

"Right. Second question—how much does a cheeseburger cost?"

Again, my response is quick and certain, since I can quote the whole Burger King menu verbatim. I respond, "$1.19."

"Correct! Question number 3—who is the bully of the Beytien boys?"

Now, I know where he's going with this question, because he doesn't like his younger brother. So I say, "Josh, we do not have any bullies in our family."

"WRONG! The answer is Zachary. Question number 4—who is the funny one of the Beytien boys?"

Again, I know where he is going with this question. I respond, "Oh, Joshua, that would definitely be you."

"RIGHT! Final Question." He pauses. "Why do you love me?"

At this point, I begin to cry and almost have to pull the car over. After all that has gone on between us today, he ends his tirade with this question? So I say, "Because you're my favorite Joshua in the whole world."

"Right. I guess you're the real mom."

And I am. A REAL mom. At least to the three wild, crazy, quirky, fabulous boys in my house. And like every "real" mom, my job doesn't end when they head off to college or turn 18. In reality, my job as the real mom will continue for my boys for many years to come.

We are navigating a new phase of life with our sons. Adulthood is upon them. I'm learning my newest set of rules, federal laws, and lingo. Just when I think I can't fill my brain with anymore acronyms, I sit in a meeting with Vocational Rehabilitation staff and there are so many letters flying around the room that I wonder if they are actually speaking in English or Text-Speak.

Writing a book means that at some point, you stop writing. But my life with my boys hasn't ended. And it definitely won't end as neatly as a mystery or historical fiction novel. I'm certain that Joshua will say something outrageously funny tomorrow and I'll wish I had added the story as a chapter. My boys will change and progress and I will change and progress.

I hope the stories I've told, and the strategies I've shared have sparked an idea, a chuckle, or a tear in recognition of our similarities. Maybe we'll get to meet someday, swap stories of self-stim, or crazy food jags. And then we can swap stories about our kids!

APPENDIX

Inclusion of Student with Autism Diversity Lesson Plan

This discussion should be modified not only to fit the age of the students in the classroom, but also to the child's specific disability. Depending upon age, some students need to have a word associated with the disability (autism or Asperger's syndrome) but typically this is not important until ages seven or older. The key issue for the presentation is to highlight the positive skills of the child, and discuss how we are all the same, yet different. If the inclusion student is non-verbal, hearing impaired, etc., this is a good time not only to describe behavior as communication, but also to give the children specific ways to react to the behaviors—what to say to a child who screams, how to model appropriate language, etc.

The impact of this lesson has been tremendous and far-reaching. I have presented this lesson plan to students as young as four and five, who remember what I have said when they are seven or eight. Young students tend to accept a child with disabilities much easier than older students do. The students love to share what they like/dislike as part of the presentation and enjoy knowing what the inclusion student enjoys. This is a perfect opportunity for all professionals involved to keep a discreet list of preferences that match the inclusion student in order to facilitate socialization around a favored activity. Everyone, from principals to teachers, parents, and professionals have enjoyed this lesson immensely. The key is flexibility and understanding of the inclusion student.

WHO IS _____?

Goal: Children will be able to accept students with disabilities in their classroom, understand the concept of same/different and recognize that we are all the same yet we are all different. Children will be empowered to ask questions of adults and others regarding the inclusion student.

Equipment/Materials: small set of dominoes, large mural paper and pens, or chalk and chalkboard.

Preparation: Advance preparation should include a meeting with parents of the inclusion student to discuss their participation comfort level.

- Determine whether the parents are comfortable participating and leading the discussion of their child. If not, facilitate their answers to some questions that might be posed by the other students.

- Ensure that answers are correct regarding the inclusion student's likes, dislikes, strengths, behaviors, etc.

- Discuss parental concerns and clarify how they prefer to describe their child.

- Take particular note of the words used, and ensure their use in presentation, especially if the parents are not leading the presentation.

- Notify all appropriate personnel of the meeting time, including the principal, speech pathologist, aide, occupational therapist, and any other school professional who will be working with the child both within the classroom environment and in other environments.

- Discuss an alternate activity outside the classroom for the student who is to be discussed.

Procedure:

1. Introduce parents and any other school professional who might not be familiar to the students.

2. Begin by asking the children if they know who _____ is. Depending upon when in the school year this is done, some students may need to be reminded of the student's name.

3. Tell the students that today we are going to talk about _____ and need their help.

4. Ask two adults to come to the front of the room. (You can use older students, but in younger classrooms, adults work best.) Ask the children if they can tell you something that is the same about the two adults. If this is a difficult concept, use the words "match" or "alike" and give a prompt answer

to facilitate. Write approximately three to five of the student responses on chalkboard or mural paper.

5. Now ask the students to tell you something that is different about the two adults. Follow the above procedure. Highlight answers again, emphasizing that they can see with their eyes what is the same and what is different.

6. Ask if they have noticed anything that is the same about _____ and themselves. Write answers again on the board, prompting if needed.

7. Ask the children if they have noticed anything different about _____ and themselves. This is the time for flexibility! The answers may be difficult for parents to hear, and sensitivity should be given to both parents and students. All answers are correct! Do not explain or discuss the answers just yet, simply write them down and encourage answers.

8. Depending upon the child's disability and challenges, discussion should follow with adult direction about the nature of "different" not meaning wrong, bad, or scary. If the child's classmates have highlighted behaviors that are different from theirs, discuss what the behaviors communicate for the child with autism (e.g., anger, unhappiness, etc.) Parents who are not leading the discussion might join in telling the students that their child wasn't always this way, or has made great progress, etc. This helps the other children know that the child with autism will learn and grow during the school year, just like they will learn and grow.

9. Line the dominoes up on a table and ask the children if they know what they are. (Most do!) Tell them that these dominoes

are like their brain. When you tell your brain something (such as say Hello to someone) your brain tells the rest of you to respond. Knock over the dominoes while saying this to mimic brain pathways responding to input. Then line the dominoes up again. Tell the students that _____ has a brain just like theirs, except it is slightly different. Move approximately five dominoes out from the middle of the line, and shift them to another part of the table. Explain that when _____ hears "Hello" (Knock over the first domino) his/her brain sometimes does not get the message to the rest of their body (the dominoes will stop in the middle, leaving some dominoes standing) Tell the students that all the people in the room (list the professionals and assistants standing around) are going to help _____ put his/her dominoes back in place.

10. Explain that _____ is as smart as they are and has all the same dominoes; however, _____ 's dominoes have been rearranged and sometimes move slower than other students' dominoes do. But the students can help _____ move those brain dominoes!

11. Ask the parents (if in the room) what _____ enjoys doing and list the activities on the board. Ask the parents other typical questions such as what the child likes/ dislikes to eat, what toys are preferred, favorite activities, etc. Finish by asking the parents if _____ likes to have friends. (The answer should be yes!)

12. Ask the children how many of them like to have friends. (All hands should go up!) Then tell them that this shows that they are the SAME as _____. Go down the list of the

student's like/dislikes and repeat the procedures of "How many of you like _____?" As hands go up, remind them that this means they can be a friend to _____ , because they like/dislike the same things.

13. End with thanking all the students for listening and learning how to be a great friend to _____. Depending upon the age of the students, ask if there are any other questions that they would like to ask the parents or teacher.

RESOURCES

There are a significant number of really good books, manuals, websites, and blogs these days that can inform and support anyone connected with autism. While it is impossible to read everything, I try to read as much as I can. Below are the books that I have found most helpful.

When your child has been diagnosed with autism ...

Ten Things Every Child with Autism Wishes You Knew by
Ellen Notbohm

A Parent's Guide to Autism by Charles Hart

Facing Autism by Lynn Hamilton

*1001 Great Ideas for Teaching and Raising Children with
Autism or Asperger's* by Veronica Zysk and Ellen Notbohm

When you're trying to decide on an intervention or treatment ...

*Autism Spectrum Disorders: Interventions and Treatments for
Children and Youth* by Richard Simpson

Behavioral Interventions for Young Children with Autism
edited by Catherine Maurice

When you want to focus on social skills ...

The Social Skills Picture Book by Dr. Jed Baker (there is a high school version also)

Anything written by Michelle Garcia Winner

Navigating the Social World by Jeannette McAfee

The Incredible 5-point Scale by Kari Dunn Buron and Mitzi Curtis

The Hidden Curriculum by Brenda Smith Myles

When a particular behavior is overwhelming your life ...

Positive Strategies for Students with Behavior Problems by Crimmins, Farrell, Smith, and Bailey

Parent Survival Manual edited by Eric Schopler

When you have questions about Individual Education Plans ...

How Well Does Your IEP Measure Up? By Diane Twactman-Cullen

The Everyday Advocate by Areva Martin, Esq.

Autism: Asserting Your Child's Right to a Special Education by David Sherman

When you want to explain autism to your extended family and others ...

Souls: Beneath and Beyond Autism by Sharon Rosenbloom and Thomas Basalmo

Temple Grandin: an HBO Documentary Film

The Curious Incident of the Dog in the Night-time by Mark Haddon (a fiction novel)

Mockingbird by Kathryn Erskine (a fiction novel, also suitable for teens)

When you are looking for resources in your area or moving ...

www.autism-society.org

www.autismspeaks.org

When you want a daily hit of humor about autism ...

Facebook page: The Autism Life

INDEX

anesthesia, 258–259
creative solutions, 257–258
connection with physician, 256
and meltdowns, 261
Health care, strategies for managing
ask questions, 261
have another adult, 260–261
limit interaction, 260
practice, 262–263
precautions, recovery room,
261–262
records, 261
sensory processing difficulties,
263
visuals, 262
Hippotherapy, 88–89
Holidays
Christmas, 197–199
Halloween, 196–197
Thanksgiving, 197
Holidays, strategies for
awareness, promotion of, 200
schedule, 200
solitude, providing for, 200
visuals, 199
Holiday-Wiley, Liane, 193

I

IEP. *See* Individual Education Plans
(IEP)
Individual Education Plans (IEP)
antagonistic environment, 11
and federal education law, 111
grief cycle, 112–113
Individual Education Plan (IEP),
strategies for developing
collaboration, 115

focus, 114–115
forward thinking, 114
positiveness, 116
practical tips for parents, 117–
118
practical tips for teachers, 116–
117
proactiveness, 114
understanding, 115
unity, 115
Interventions
changing, 84
choosing, 82
education, 89
false cures, 81–82
floortime, 86–87
love, 84
method and format, 83
Intervention, strategies for
Applied Behavioral Analysis
Program (ABA), 85–86
auditory integration therapy,
87–88
hippotherapy, 88–89
Lovass method, 85–86
philosophy of, 85
speech therapy, 86

L

Language development
"autism sounds," 27–28
myths about, 25–26
Lord, Dr. Catherine, 139, 214, 215,
256
Lovaas method, 85–86
Love, expressing and understanding
physical touch, 66

appropriate language, 54–55
appropriate vs. inappropriate
     connections, 57
physical changes, 52–53
sexuality, emerging, 51–52
social skills, 53–54
Puberty, strategies for managing
     developmental delay vs. physical
          delay, 55
     honor "no," 56–57
     public vs. private, 56
     sexual relationship rules, 56
Pyramid Therapy, 82

R

Refrigerator Mothers, 83
Residential placement
     adjustments to, 185
     aggressive behavior, 178–180
     changes in routine as a result of,
          183–185
     conflict about, 181–182, 186
     as intervention, 180–182
     necessity for, 178–180
     self-recrimination, 186
     trauma of, 183
Residential placement, strategies for
     decision
     emotion vs. fact, 188
     intuition, 187
     full disclosure, 188
     second guessing, 188
     trusted advisors, 187

S

S.A.D. *See* Seasonal Affective
     Disorder (S.A.D.)

Seasonal Affective Disorder (S.A.D.),
     61
Self-stimulating behaviors
     (stimming)
     and active engagement, 31–32
     and development, 28
     EEG for, 29–31
     with extended family, 167
     with health care, 257
     and sensory processing, 28–29
     shopping, 248
     and skill increases, 28
Self-stimulating behaviors
     (stimming), strategies for
     managing
     eliminating downtime, 34
     exercise, 33
     shaping vs. eliminating, 32–33
Sense of humor, 209–211
Sense of humor, strategies for
     maintaining
     perspective, 212
     social media, 212
Sense of self, parents, 219–220
Sense of self, strategies for retaining
     focus, 222
     hobbies, 221
     schedule, 221
     sleep, 221
     support group, 222
Shopping
     attitudes of others, 237–238
     environment, 236
     stress overload, 238
     visual schedule, 236
Shopping, strategies for
     limits, 239–240
     online shopping, 240

Extend teaching & learning with these great resources!

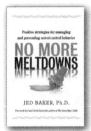
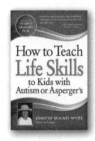

Be sure to check out this new acclaimed series by Kathy Labosh!

Support self-awareness and tackle unique challenges with these children's books!

My Friend with Autism

This book's vivid illustrations and charming story-line will foster tolerance and understanding among peers, while the printable coloring pages on the included CD will enlighten and engage learners!

ISBN 9781935274186 | $14.95

Sensitive Sam

Sam is frustrated by his over-sensitivity. But with occupational therapy, a "sensory diet," and the love of his family, Sam concludes that "now I LIKE doing lots of things I used to hate to do!"

ISBN 9781932565867 | $14.95

Ellie Bean, the Drama Queen

Ellie Bean tends to overreact when things don't go her way (a situation all too familiar to author/mom/special education teacher Jennie Harding). Join Ellie as she learns how to cope with her feelings and keep calm!

ISBN 9781935567271 | $9.95

Picky, Picky Pete

Written by an occupational therapist, this picture book is a must-have! Pete finds his clothes uncomfortable and can't stand "paint, soap, and things with lumps." He and his mom learn to navigate his challenges together.

ISBN 9781935567219 | $14.95

Available at fine retailers everywhere and at www.FHautism.com.

FUTURE HORIZONS INC.